YOU ARE MY SISTER, NOT MY COMPETITION

STOP COMPETING WITH OTHER WOMEN AND LEARN TO APPRECIATE THEM.

J.A. HUGGINS

CONTENTS

ISBN: 978-1-7372191-0-1 (paperback)

ISBN: 978-1-7372191-1-8 (ebook)

This book is dedicated to my family.
My strength, my heart and my motivation

My mother Denise Huggins —
A better mother never lived

My nieces —
The innocence within each of you inspires me.
May you always be righteously guided, protected and loved.

And to my father, S. Morris —
Gone far too soon.

And my brother Naldo Swanday Huggins—
Your essence will forever linger and your memory will never depart from
my heart. My lion hearted brother and friend,
I will love you to the very end.

INTRODUCTION

I can only write about what I know, what I've experienced, and what I imagine. The expressions I'm making here are authentic, and they are my own. I don't have all the answers, but I hope to broaden your awareness. At the end of this book, you must determine for yourself who you are and who you want to become. You will have to find the strength to confront the source of your own insecurities and resentments, to improve your own state of mind. Remember that you are not alone. I'm just a woman who's been through some shit. That said, I would rather be the kind of person who adds to the cup of others, rather than taking from it.

It's not easy to be vulnerable or to admit one's role in perpetuating a problem. I know this, and you know this. I'm prepared to take you to the place where my pain lives, to show you how it took shape and how it almost took my life. But this is not a sad story. You see, pain doesn't appreciate being ignored. It demands to be felt. I tried going around my pain for years. I tried existing as though it was not a part of my life. It was only when I decided to go through it that I finally came out on the other side — the side where I wake up every day grateful and happy to be alive, with a compelling desire to do something good.

Ever since I was a little girl, I've had a front row seat to the ever-present issue of female rivalry. Family members, friends, strangers, politicians, and of course, radio and television. I was bombarded with representations of unhealthy and unproductive female competition — the kind that makes you anxious, depressed, insecure, and jealous. At ten years old, I was thrust into the world of pageantry in the small village where I grew up — a beautiful Caribbean Island called St. Kitts — and there was no shortage of competition. Between the ages of ten and nineteen I had entered nine pageants, winning seven. Every detail of these pageants was meticulously planned and rehearsed until it was perfect. In real life, we can plan all we want, but there are rarely rehearsals, hardly any do-overs. Often, one shot is all we get.

My reality was painful. Every pageant bred new hatred and resentment toward me. The most hurtful part was that the worst of it came from those closest to me. The more popular I became among strangers, the more unpopular I was to those I loved. The more I tried to please those around me, the more I disappeared into a dark and lonely place within. All I had was the stage, and the attention and validation it offered me. It became my choice of drug. Whenever the momentum would die down from one pageant, I eagerly sought out the next. That ever-present and ever-expanding void had a firm grip on me and I was losing the battle. Once the high wore off, I was forced to face harsh truths — about myself, those around me, and the source of my loneliness.

At first, I didn't understand why some girls didn't like me. There was no preparation or rehearsal for that. I was taught that to win, I needed to make everyone watching love me. Year after year I was told:

"You have to make them love you."

"If they don't love you, you don't win."

"If they don't think you're the best, you won't win."

"If they don't like you more than all the other girls, you can't win."

Off the stage, my haters had become the audience and judging panel that I needed to sway in my favor, or so I thought. I tried being everything to everyone. I compared myself to other women. I picked myself apart and then resented the women who I thought were better than me. I didn't feel I was good enough. I thought if I could only win one more pageant, they'd have to see me then. I wanted to please everyone and be perfect, but I couldn't. When pressure built and rumors threatened that perfection, my life almost tragically ended.

When you've looked everywhere else for answers, prayed to God to help you find a way out, but you keep looking around and can't seem to find the answer, look to the place where you have not yet searched — yourself. The answer is within you, as it was within me all along. The moment I began looking inward, it became obvious that the external factors were just a bunch of noisy distractions.

The right women began lining themselves up in my life. My own experiences brought me out of my darkness. God used the focus of my pain as the tool to help me overcome that pain. Women were not in fact the source of my suffering — that was a deeper wound, which impaled my heart and mind much earlier in life. We all have a reason we do the things we do, and are the way we are. I needed to forgive, but I also needed to be forgiven to move on.

You are My Sister, Not My Competition has haunted me for years. The title has refused to let me go since it made its way into my head eight years ago. I'm not a therapist; I'm not a doctor or a teacher. I'm a woman who has seen enough female competition. I know all too well the devastating effects it has on an individual, a family, a society, and the world. This is not who we are. We are strong, compassionate, and nurturing creations. We don't want to spend our lives comparing ourselves to others, constantly criticizing, playing judge, jury, and executioner to other women. We are all uniquely and beautifully flawed. We have more in common than our pride sometimes allows us to admit. We can change this dynamic. We can be the example of a female force built on understanding, compassion, and love, rather than one divided by differences, intolerance, and hate.

The dynamic of unhealthy female competition needs to shift. Its results have continued to dictate the way women feel about each other and ourselves. Insecurities have increased and self-esteem has plummeted. Friendships have been ruined. Depression and hate have made their way into the lives of even the youngest among us, and the outcome has too often been fatal.

This needs to change, and we can change it. We can migrate from a place of comparison and judgment to a place of understanding. We must allow ourselves to be open, to listen and understand what makes each of us who we are. The paths that led us here may be different, but compassion can reveal how much more we have in common.

We can achieve this with one word: love. By learning to love ourselves and each other, by being grateful instead of jealous, by being compassionate instead of hateful, we establish peace, love, and acceptance. It becomes easier to carry that out into the world. The amazing news is that it's possible.

This is my journey. This book is not only for you; it is also for me. It is a constant aid in my everyday growth to becoming a better woman, a better friend, and a better person. Are you tired of the games, the competition, and of comparing yourself and being compared to other women? Are you tired of feeling like you're not living up to society's expectations of beauty and perfection, tired of ridiculing yourself and other women, and tired of the jealousies and pettiness within your friend circles? Are you tired of competing over the affection and attention of men? Are you tired of trying to be someone you're not, because you're afraid to show people who you are? Tired of not being able to trust and lean on other women? Tired of having to downplay your successes to avoid making other women feel bad? Tired of wondering why some women don't like you?

Take this journey to self-awareness, empowerment, redemption, forgiveness, and love with me. We can do this together. Allow me to share with you the lessons I have learned and the life-changing habits that I have put in place. I still work on improving every day. I am not a teacher or a philosopher, but I hope that my experiences will serve as a street light on the dark road to your own truth. The choice to open your mind and your heart to the possibility of a better reality is yours. I can only guide you to recognize what is inside yourself. To be good to others, we must first learn to be good to ourselves. We must first believe that there is good within us, then draw that out by cultivating the best parts of who we are, because we are magnanimous.

ONE
THE COMPETITION

"Girl skedaddle, run faster, hurry and pass me the relay stick!" my teammate yells as she bounces and leaps about.

I jet down the track with the wind tearing through my flushed, freckled cheeks. Finally, I come to a halt. It's the finishing line.

"Whew, oh my God, we won!" The words of sweet victory leave my hot, almost breathless mouth.

I loved running and playing netball as a young girl growing up on my beautiful Caribbean Island of St. Kitts — untouched and more breathtaking than you can imagine. Lush mountainous hills cascade across the horizon as though they're putting on a show, much like an elegant dance to the vibrations of the wind. Stunning blue ocean waters crash on what I can only describe as diamond dusted, brown sandy shores. The air is so clean, you can almost taste the decadence. I am proud to come from such a veritable paradise.

Preparing for our sports days was always heaps of fun. We would rush out of classes early to practice for the different sporting events. We had everything from traditional 100-meter sprints to 8000-meter drawn out runs. Then, there were the cool races. The biggest challenge of all during these was actually keeping a straight face, trying not to die with laughter before reaching the finishing line. One of our races included placing a lime in a metal spoon and speed walking to the finishing line. Another was shuffling down the 100-meter track, threading a tiny needle, and then hauling ass back to the finishing line. Of all the races, the relay races in elementary school were my favorite. I loved the teamwork required to snatch a win. It was always more fun seeing so many of my friends on the track — not to mention the pressure being lifted if you were not the fastest runner.

I was always so intimidated standing on the starting line of a 100-meter dash, but not for relay races. There was something about knowing that the other girls on my team had my back, and that I had theirs. We all shared in the outcome, whatever it was. I was pretty decent at sprints, despite almost peeing my pants a few times. The starting gun would fire off, and it would take a second or two for my heart to re-enter my chest. With sprints, every second counted, but the relay races had a different setup. I was never the starter; I was usually the finisher or somewhere in the middle, and never fussed over what position would draw the most attention. There was no anger if I wasn't the one bringing it home to the finish line. I was quite content to be part of a team, especially with my friends. Even at that age, I understood the power of combining strengths to overcome weaknesses, and the importance of working together toward one goal. The entire team celebrated winning and each loss was felt by the entire team. If someone dropped the stick, picked it up, and still won the race, we were all winners.

Now, if that same someone dropped the stick, and we ended up losing the race, that's the entire team's loss too, right? Wrong! Now it's that person's fault alone. The team was with you until you stopped benefiting them. Team relationships didn't come without their trials. There was always that individual whose sentiments were, "I am the reason we won and you are the reason we lost."

The way the boys operated intrigued and confused me at the same time. I never understood how they could compete against each other, pulverize their opponent, then sprawl around, laughing and eating snacks idly, like everything was cool. When the girls lost, our tropics turned into the frigid arctic. It was iciness and death stares for at least three days, and that was a long time in girl time. But we would certainly grow out of these habits, as age brings maturity, right? There was no need to be alarmed. Or was there?

SO, WHAT IS THIS COMPETITION?

Difficult to work with.

Dramatic. Catty. Undermining, judgmental and fake.

Competitive, jealous, backbiting, and untrustworthy.

These are only a few of the plethora of terms used to describe women.

We have placed women into a faction system based on superficial criteria such as appearance, status, wealth, education, religion, culture, attitudes, and sexuality. From the time I was old enough to understand conflict, I had already observed (and was sometimes part of) the culture of female competition. No, not competition for academic achievements, sports, or better jobs. I'm not referring to good old healthy competition. I'm speaking of that abysmal, vain, validation-seeking, need-to-be-perceived-as-better-than other women competition. That crush-you-like-a-quivering-bug kind of competition — the animalistic, primal instinct and desire to feel dominant.

I love healthy competition, and I encourage it. Women should have outlets for their natural competitive sides, as men do. Women need healthy and productive ways to release that aggression. We should not meet it with shame, but it ought to be accomplished without creating conflict and rivalry.

The level of unhealthy competition seems to have gotten fiercer. The arena has widened to become a pervasive spectacle of female domination — usually by slander, slaughter, and flat-out hate of other women. I should know; for a long time, I felt I couldn't trust other women. From my personal experiences, they were boastful and devoid of humility — conceited, underhanded, conniving, hateful, backstabbers. I couldn't distinguish between them anymore, so I began distrusting them all. After years of disappointment and verbal abuse by an older female cousin, I became that which I despised the most. I became one of those women, drowning myself in the competition. I became obsessed and even depressed over my existence.

Women have given life to these stereotypes with the derogatory labels we put on each other. Women are judging each other before even giving one another a chance. We look at their clothes and hair, their bodies, the way they speak, the jobs they have, the homes they live in, the money they make, and the cars they drive. We create these classifications and comparisons according to where we see ourselves, and who we've convinced ourselves that we are. It's warfare — searching for someone's weakness, not to help them, but to attack what or who they care for most. It's a tit for tat game of who can hurt whom the most. We attack each other's children, spouses, families, friends, careers, religious beliefs, and sexuality — nothing is off limits. All this is to claim a victory over another.

We'll curse other women, dragging their names and reputations through the mud over a man — a man who vowed to be faithful, but couldn't keep his promise. We'll wage war on each other without giving a second thought to the fallout. The collateral damage caused by pettiness can create a handicap in another person's life. It can change the trajectory of who a person might become, altering how they think, feel, and act toward other people. Worse is the dangerous and frightening society we're creating for young girls and boys to inherit. We're leaving them defenseless, without the proper tools to navigate this destructive terrain. Young girls are suffering and struggling in silence because they don't trust us as women. Can we really blame them when we don't even trust each other?

WE'RE CAUGHT UP, AND IT'S DESTROYING US

Before we can establish them anywhere else, we need to first establish equal rights amongst ourselves as women. How can we expect the rest of the world to see the value in us if we can't even see the value in ourselves and each other? How can we expect a society to rally with us and support us if we can't rally with and support each other?

Visualize the type of woman you wish other women would be to you, and start being that woman to others. Allow your actions and attitudes to inspire women to be better to themselves and to each other. Love who other women are, while also loving yourself. There is no sacrifice of your self-worth required. You don't have to hide, be ashamed or afraid of who you are, or think less of yourself to think more of others. It is so easy to dismiss the problem. We'd rather run away from the issue, because confronting it means we each have to confront the source of our problems. You may think that there is no way out. Anchor your thoughts to all the things that you don't have — all the things you feel you are not. You compare yourself to all the people you think have achieved their happiness, and you feel late and lost. It can be a terrifying thing, but I'm here to tell you that it doesn't have to be a lonely road through that hell. Just keep going, keep fighting, keep making the effort every day to do better and to be a better person.

I spent the former parts of my life existing without living. I handed the keys to my success and happiness off to the world. Whatever the world said I needed in order to be happy was what I went after. Whoever it said I should look like to feel beautiful was who I aimed to emulate. Whomever others said I needed to be to receive love and acceptance was who I was desperate to become.

I thought I was the only woman feeling like this. No one talked about it or admitted it. No woman I knew or had met ever dared to say that they were watching the actions of other women before proceeding in their own life. Everyone carried on, unsuccessfully attempting to convince others that what they were doing was original and unique.

I took a step back, and I asked myself, "Is that truly possible?" I wanted to be one of those women who didn't follow, who didn't look at what anyone else was doing, who did not care what others thought of her, and didn't mind being put out of the race. That's what it felt like — a race. But where was everyone in such a hurry to get to?

I couldn't help but observe the society of women, exclaiming their liberation and individuality. Yet many seemed hell-bent on looking and acting the same way, accumulating the same material things, and even chasing after the same men. The worst part was that each woman's goals were being set according to what the next woman had, how fast she got it, and how she achieved it . The competition began long before you or I were born. I wanted to think of myself as special, above it all somehow, as though I was exempt from temptation and wrongdoing.

I was a girl, and the competition seduced me in the same way it did other women - until I looked around and saw the severity of women comparing themselves and their lives to others'. I saw the depressive state that women and girls were existing in. They were deeply insecure, never content with what they had, and only focused on what they wanted to have. They were going into debt living above their financial means to maintain a certain perception, rejecting the help of others for fear of looking dependent and, consequently, not independent enough. Health and family were sacrificed to achieve unrealistic expectations of physical beauty. Women were neglecting their children, their homes, and themselves in pursuit of fame and status; none were truly happy with who they were, hating and envying women who seemed to have it all. Young girls hated themselves and other girls over petty jealousies, harming themselves and each other because they didn't feel like they were enough. I knew all too well what that felt like, and I didn't want to be swallowed down any further.

IT DOESN'T HAVE TO BE THAT WAY.

Aren't you tired of watching women hurt each other? Aren't you fed up with your friends talking behind your back and not knowing who to trust? Don't you want to feel good about other women's successes, especially when that success breaks the glass ceiling and paves a way for you and others to get through? Aren't you tired of feeling like a hypocrite for holding on to grudges, backbiting, and being jealous of other women? I was, so I did something about it. I knew I couldn't point all fingers at other women, though. One had to be pointed right back at me, because I was part of the problem, even while complaining about that problem. I fell into the trap and believed the stereotype that women just can't help themselves, that we are just competitive creatures, even more so than men. I think I believed it because it gave me an excuse. If that was true, though, why were there women who weren't jealous of each other? Why were there women who were fighting to help other women succeed, even ahead of themselves ? I knew it didn't need to be this way.

Only women can truly understand what other women go through. Only other women can appreciate what it takes to overcome the things we endure and survive. When I realized this, I gained a newfound level of respect, admiration, and love. To find myself, I had to admit that I was lost. To figure out a better way, I had to admit that what I was doing was wrong.

You can change the dynamic of your female relationships and the way you deal with other women. It takes self-reflection (and even a little hindsight) to understand why —why do you feel the way you do about certain women? Why do some women evoke such jealousies and hatred within you, and why is it so hard to be genuinely happy for other women doing well? Take a step back and think about those demeaning words, how often you've used them when referring to another woman, and whether they have ever been used against you. Pay attention to the emotions stirring as you focus on that for a moment.

We have much more in common than we'd like to admit. It doesn't matter what culture, color, or creed we are. Once we remove the blinders of social stereotypes, hate, and envy from our eyes, this becomes much easier to recognize and appreciate. We are never more effective than when we come together as one tightly woven fabric. The actions of some amazing women guided me to discovering something even greater within myself.

TWO
INNOCENCE INTERRUPTED

MY MOM AND DAD SPLIT UP WHEN I WAS THREE YEARS OLD, AND MY father moved to an island called St. Maarten. My parents had two incredible children together. I was one of them, of course, and my older brother Jay was the other. My father had eight other children from previous relationships. My brother and I were the only full siblings of the bunch. Talk about sowing your oats, huh?

My parents never got married; when they separated, my dad took my brother and left me with my mom. He had raised none of his other children, so I guess that was as good a time as any for him to start. At three years old, the effects of the separation came on slowly, but it eventually became obvious how much that single decision changed me.

My father choosing to take my brother instead of me planted the seed for my competitiveness. The desire to seek his validation and prove that I would have added value to his life, if only he'd chosen to take me instead of my brother, was growing stronger than anyone (including myself) could have imagined.

My first experience of rejection and the spark that ignited my mission to prove my worth came from a single decision my father made, and one which he didn't look back from. Still, I had a fierce love for him. As children, we often have this impeccable ability to see the best parts of those we love, and choose to toss the rest. I was a child in every way — innocent and hopeful. How could I have understood and made sense of everything I was feeling? I became obsessed with proving that I was good enough, that I was worthy of being chosen. I was ready to do whatever it took to get his attention and affection back. It's funny how we sometimes don't realize we've been crippled until we actually decide to pull ourselves up and walk.

One could say it's easy to blame our insecurities and fears on our childhoods to avoid taking responsibility for our adult decisions. I, however, find no ease in that reality. We should protect children, as they are innocent until corrupted. The ideas, principles, values, and habits that create the makeup of who we are all cement themselves into our psyches as children. You cannot afford to overlook the beginning and simply skip to the middle or the end; the story just won't make sense. Think about the first time you really felt like you had something to prove, something you felt you had to compete for.

KIDS AND ADULTS CAN BE MEAN

It became blisteringly clear when I started elementary school that I didn't have what others considered a complete and stable family. Other kids constantly reminded me that my father wasn't around and that we had little money, teaching me how brutal they could be. My mom worked tirelessly to take care of her kids. I was eight years old the first time another little girl hurled at me, "Your mother cleans other people's big houses and you live in a little shack."

I looked to teachers for help, as children are taught to do, but rarely found any. Once in a classroom, a teacher requested that all students provide a telephone number to contact parents. She strutted over to me like a well-built robot on a mission. If only I'd had a remote control to demobilize her. I hoped she would recognize the trembling in my body, but she didn't.

"Teacher, my mom doesn't have a phone," I whispered.

She demanded that I speak up.

"I don't have a phone, but I can give you my aunt's number instead."

I can still remember the laughter screeching in my ears: "Aha ha, she can't afford a phone! "

"Be quiet, everybody. Stop teasing her," she said, very cavalierly . Then she asked, "When will your mother have a phone?"

Are you kidding me? Was she so dense that she couldn't see what was happening? I mumbled that I didn't know. Who would've thought that not having something as simple as a telephone could make me feel so inferior among my peers at such a young age?

I lashed out one lunch period at being called a bastard child by another little girl. I didn't know what the word meant. All I knew was how it made me feel — crappy.

I took it to a teacher who, without a single attempt to console me, explained, "Well, your parents didn't get married so the word can't offend you. That's what it means, even if you don't like the way it sounds."

Then she told three other teachers about the incident, seeking their validation for her response. I stood back and painfully listened as they discussed my parents' marital status in judgment.

At that moment, I despised being a kid who had to be respectful to her teachers at all times. My tongue was wobbling in my mouth. My teeth fought to keep that tongue trapped behind them. It was burning like sulphuric acid, desperate to be spewed out at her. I held my tongue. Hell, I'm certain I bit my tongue. I couldn't talk back, because my mother taught me better than that. The last thing I needed was for them to say that I had no home training.

I gave up on trusting that the teachers could do anything to help me, especially after I would overhear them talking behind each other's backs. The gossip was intense and brutal — definitely not child's play.

Even students weren't exempt from their secret sessions of gossip.

"She's going to get pregnant before she ever finishes high school."

"I doubt that one will even make it to high school."

"His mother should focus more on her child and stop partying every weekend."

"Well, it's no wonder she's so spoiled. Look at her mother."

How could I trust them? I didn't.

NO MATTER WHERE IT COMES FROM

We don't always remember names, places, or even faces, but we never forget how we felt. The things that happen to us as children, and how we and those we trust choose to respond, can play a huge role in who we become as adults. Young girls are dismissed for telling the truth in their lives. Their families and communities label them outcasts for revealing the secrets that crush them from the inside. There are so many disenfranchised young women around the world, and so many who feel less important than others because of the color of their skin, where they come from, their religion, poverty, and social status. I knew girls as a teen who experimented with drugs, alcohol, and sex even before I knew the dangers of such things. It doesn't make a difference whether you're a seventeen-year-old or a thirty-year-old reading this. Women and young girls are being taken every day against their will. Girls are being forced to leave school in some places, and in others they are denied an education. Whether abandoned by a parent, abused, neglected, or bullied - if we do not address properly those girls' issues and traumas, it's only a matter of time before we're forced to confront the consequences.

We may pace through our lives thinking that we're alright, burying the pain or trying to convince ourselves that we're unaffected by it, but we're only fooling ourselves. The pain and resentments only lay dormant until something inevitably triggers all those memories and the emotions that go with them. Have you ever encountered a person and initially given them a hard time because they reminded you of someone from your past who hurt you? The popular girl who made fun of you, the female relative who belittled or abused you, the mom who neglected or beat you, the teacher who made you feel dumb, the friend who made you feel unpretty, the person who made you feel too fat or too skinny, or the person who sexually violated you?

When we interrupt a girl's innocence and taint the life she perceives as happy, it is very easy for her to blame herself. Girls, too young to understand or cope, take those feelings and tuck them away, or make them the focus and impetus to their fears, insecurities, jealousies, anxiety, anger, resentment, and competi-tiveness. Like it or not, they become the bricks that create the foundation of those girls' lives. Our compassion, patience, faith, resilience, strength, and loyalty are all characteristics that come from what we have been exposed to. Our childhoods are where our principles take shape.

LEARN FROM WHAT YOU CANNOT UNDO

Now that you're a grown woman, you have more control than you did as a child. You choose how to react, if you should react, and when you should react to situations. You've experienced some-thing in your life that didn't make you feel good, even if you had an amazing childhood free of any psychological trauma. Maybe you're even a mom yourself now. Examine your own behavior. Is there something you're still holding on to? Are you still fighting battles that began in your childhood? I recall countless arguments as a child among the surrounding adults. If we are going to expose young girls and children to unhealthy confrontations and arguing, then we must expose them to healthy resolutions. We cannot undo or unsee the things that the adults in our lives exposed us to, but we can learn from them and do better. Women talking trash behind each other's backs and then smiling at their subjects' faces isn't inherent, it's taught through the examples of surrounding women. The mean streak, the bullying, and the teasing from other girls was learned behavior.

We can't focus on the examples given to us in our childhoods now. We have to be the examples. Listen to other women, young or old. A girl should never feel voiceless or invisible. Give a young girl or another woman someone to trust. There is nothing more terri-fying than feeling like you have nowhere to turn for help. Teach by example; show respect and have good manners. Stop the name calling and show outward affection and appreciation for other women, because you understand how strong we have all had to be to make it this far. Don't be so quick to ridicule others and compare successes or failures. Be mindful of your behavior, because there is always some little girl looking at you. Instead of debating whose responsibility it is, let's just accept the responsibility with pride when opportunities arise, be it a parent, teacher, best friend, sister, coach, or a complete stranger. If we want young women to be better, then we must do better and be better examples for them.

When things happen to us, especially as children, we may lack the capacity to comprehend why. All we know is how it makes us feel. Once we're old enough, it becomes extremely important to make peace with the things that we feel disrupted our innocence. You may never fully understand why, because you can't force the readiness or willingness of others to explain their actions to you. Sometimes that person may not even understand their own actions, which makes it impossible for them to offer you any closure. You can't make them apologize or feel bad. They may have moved on with their lives and never given a second thought to the damage they caused you. Sometimes the best closure is simply taking your power back. You accept that they hurt you, accept that it was not your fault and that they are not perfect, forgive them, forgive yourself if you must, protect yourself from what they've shown you they're capable of, and move on with your life.

THREE
THE GIFT AND THE CURSE

I HAVE ALWAYS LOVED MUSIC AND BEGAN SINGING IN SCHOOL AND IN church at four years old. I was using hair brushes and anything else I could find, zipping around barefoot and singing. Lord help me, I thought I was Celine Dion and Whitney Houston wrapped in a bundle and nobody could convince me otherwise. Music was an escape. It was a place where I felt free and fearless. I was quite coy, but somehow, with music, my shyness busted through the window.

I was introduced to the world of pageantry at age ten. Winning my first pageant was a gift and a curse that just seemed to keep on giving. The worst I thought of other little girls was that they were tattletales who cried when you took their stuff away. They whined when you tried forcing them to share and they teased you for not having material things. That was all before — I found out quickly what lurked behind those cute faces and pigtails. They had unseen fangs ready to draw blood at any second.

Overnight, I was being taunted for things I never thought were issues. I was what they called on the islands a "hairy breed." I had long sideburns that connected to the hair on the nape of my neck, thick eyebrows, and a little peach fuzz on my upper lip — none of which I, at ten years old, ever thought made me ugly. Now the girls were saying I looked like a boy and that I couldn't sing. They said that my mom was poor and my father didn't love me because he wasn't around.

Well, shit! I would have given that damn crown back in a heartbeat, if only to have all those words slither back to the venomous tongues from which they sprang. Just like that, they disliked me. Not because I walked differently or talked differently - nothing about me had changed. They placed a piece of metal with fake stones on my head. "A piece of metal!" I thought. The sad part was that I felt such pride in representing my school and winning that piece of metal for us all.

By the time I entered my last year in high school, I had won six pageants and joined a musical band. Things were changing around me, and it was happening far too quickly for my young mind to comprehend. The attention that pageants garnered me only made things worse. Being singled out to do things in school placed a target on my back; I joined the band to have an outlet away from all the pageantry, but they still blasted me for it. Women compared me to other singers and criticized everything from my clothes, to my dancing, to my character. When I dressed too modestly (because I was still a child) they ridiculed me for being dull. When I changed that up, they accused me of sleeping with my band mates. I didn't look right, dress right, dance right, or sing the right songs. Eventually I quit the band, and pageants just weren't fun anymore.

WHEN IT COMES FROM THOSE INSIDE

I changed because I felt like I had no control. I was desperate to convert haters into fans. Some of my family members seemed hell-bent on reminding me that no matter how many crowns I won, I was nothing. I came from nothing and I wasn't anything special. The worst was that my mom was put down quite a lot by her own relatives. They judged and ridiculed her for allowing me to enter the pageants.

What people didn't know was that I wiped my mother's tears. I watched her cry countless times. I heard her prayers as she asked for forgiveness and the guidance to do right by her children. I saw her fears, her sacrifices, her struggles, and her strengths. My mother did the best that a mother could. Even before I was born, she was fighting to protect me. She hauled ass running one day while still pregnant with me, fighting to escape the hands of my father. There were nights my mother stayed up lamenting, "I have little education, I have little money, I don't know what I'm doing! Lord, help me make the best decisions for my child." It takes humility to admit that you cannot do something on your own.

My mother is a beautiful woman with the most generous of hearts. She is the hardest worker I know. She's humble, selfless, and inspiring. She has an unwavering love and devotion for her family, despite how terrible some of them were toward her and her children. I watched the internal struggle caused by her sisters and nieces putting her down every chance they got, belittling her for not having something in her life that they did. Her own sisters were selfish and unkind toward her too many times. Anytime she shared an idea with them about advancing herself in life, they discouraged her and told her she was too late, was not intelligent enough, or didn't have enough money.

How could women be like that? How could her own blood be like that? I was very protective of my mom. I still am. Who the heck isn't? I saw the hurt and the pain she bore in silence because of their treatment toward her. It affected me at my core. I couldn't understand how she remained so loyal and giving toward them; worse than that, I couldn't fix it. If she had two tomatoes and one of my aunts wanted two, she would pretend to have three and give them to her sister. When any of my aunts would have to go out somewhere nice, they would often flood our house and go through my mom's closet, picking out the best of what she had and telling her she never goes anywhere, so she might as well give it to them. And she would. It was cringe-worthy.

I had an older female cousin who was my personal tormentor, even though I admired her and her sister. Her younger sister was slightly less abusive, but still always present and complicit in the way my cousin treated me. My mom's twin brother has two daughters, who they also seemed to take particular pleasure in emotionally and verbally abusing. They were only kind to cousins who lived abroad and would visit. They would encourage the visiting cousins not to spend time with us, and use their belittling of us as amusement. No one ever stopped them. No one ever told them we were still children, or that what they were doing was fracturing our confidence and damaging our sense of security within the family. When their mom, my aunt, passed away, my other cousins and I struggled through conflicting grief. We loved our aunt and were sad, but we resented her dismissiveness and the way she always turned a blind eye to her children's treatment of others. I looked up to them so much. They were gorgeous girls; they always wore the best clothes, new shoes, and had pretty hair and makeup. They had a lot of freedom and everyone found them very attractive. That's why I never considered jealousy as a reason for their attitudes toward me.

Back then, I couldn't make sense of it. How could the women in my family be so cruel? Still, I wanted to remain in their favor. I began overcompensating and gave them anything they asked for, even though I didn't have as much as they did. They borrowed my clothes even before I had time to wear them. I would run errands, share whatever I had, and do whatever favors they asked of me, often catching hell from my mom. All so they would be nicer to my mom and her kids. Sometimes it worked; other times, I would leave in tears, feeling like shit. I loved my cousins, and I wanted to be like them. I wanted to be liked by them, so I never complained. They were older than me and I never fought back. I instead began taking out that hurt and pain on others, becoming quarrelsome in school. If you said something about me, I was ready to curse you out. I became comfortable having negative feelings about other women.

DISAPPEARING INNOCENCE

I never expected or asked for special treatment. I just wanted to feel appreciated for going out and doing my best—trying to win for my school, my community, and then my country. Don't we all want to feel appreciated? I would even have been okay with receiving zero appreciation if only the criticisms and hate were also nonexistent, but the scale wasn't balanced, and I was a child.

"I bet she'll get pregnant. Girls like that always do before they even finish high school. I bet she already has a man."

"She probably doesn't do well in school."

"She thinks she's better than other people now. She's not even that talented or pretty."

"She's sleeping with the guys in her band."

"Who does she think she is? She doesn't come from anything. "

"She's so stuck up; I just don't like her. I hope she loses."

"She's just a nobody from the back of the land who won a few stupid shows."

They dispensed their vitriol over me like a judge handing down a prison sentence —unchanging and final. I was helpless. What could one girl do against so many? Off the stage, I was losing.

That was the beginning of my anxiety. Imagine being diagnosed with anxiety in high school and having to keep it all to yourself. I didn't fear doing anything I had rehearsed a hundred times. I didn't fear what I knew was coming. What I feared was what I didn't know. I feared not knowing what to do or how to control my feelings. Mostly, I feared being disliked and a disappointment to people, the same ones who were disappointing me. I hid my fears very well. They taught me how to smile whether or not I was happy, and to push through whether I was comfortable or not. I became skilled at both.

The innocence had faded. My thick eyebrows were no longer cute, so they thinned them out. My natural hair didn't fit the look, so they permed it. Even the shape of my legs from my years of doing sports in elementary school had become a problem.

"Too muscular-looking," they said.

I was being trained to walk, talk, think, and act like a pageant queen.

"Never allow the judges to catch you out of character. Every bit of detail matters. They are always judging you, even off the stage."

Women were preaching these lessons. We were being trained to outshine other girls. To smile in their faces and win over their trust for a Miss Congeniality vote. To win first and make friends later. It wasn't fun for me anymore — it was my teenage job, with one assignment after the other. And the only way to get fired was to lose.

The only problem with that was that I needed to win. I needed to feel alive, seen, accepted. I needed to be something more for my family; I needed my parents to be proud, and for my mom to be treated better than a second-class citizen. I needed to be the best to be somebody.

It became even more disheartening to continue doing pageants. The more I did to represent my island, the more people were hoping for my failure. Why, though? I was representing us all. I was winning for us all. Wasn't I?

I was at my wit's end after a preliminary performance at a pageant. Two of the contestants and a chaperone verbally accosted me. I'd had the absurd idea to share my hair and makeup artist with another contestant. At the last minute, she'd found out that hers would not make it, so I let her use mine. Those girls called me an idiot, told me I came from a tiny country that no one knew or cared about, and there was no way in hell that I was going to win, so I should go back to where I came from.

I wish someone had begged me to stop, begged me not to continue offering myself up for exploitation, to see it for what it was and still is. It wasn't about making friends, or establishing good morals, or building character. It was all about winning. We were spectacles of amusement offering ourselves up to be paraded around, gawked at, lusted after, and ultimately deemed most valuable. It was all a bunch of pretentious bullshit.

No one needs to prance around on a stage in a bikini to prove that they would make a good ambassador for their country, or to prove they are worthy or deserving of an academic scholarship. No one needs to be in a pretty dress and makeup to prove that they are intelligent and stand for a greater cause. What the hell does swimwear and heels have to do with world peace or helping children, anyway? It becomes easier to justify pushing half-naked women around a stage if it's promoting a cause. As long as it pulls on people's heartstrings, we allow it. Scholarship programs and opportunities to improve female relationships? Female empowerment? What a load of crap!

Nakedness, lewdness, and physical appearance do not equate to female empowerment and liberation. This needs to be exposed for the misleading and damaging message it sends to young women and men. This is part of the problem. Who and what does it benefit for women to compete based on what they look like in and out of their clothes?

We can restructure our thoughts about each other, but it begins with looking at ourselves. After experiencing so much negativity from other women, I began giving as good as I got. What didn't occur to me then was that they had reasons as valid as mine to act the way they did. I needed to get to know these women, and I mean get to know them behind the masks. I needed to look beyond the problems and the attitudes and find the source.

WORDS ARE POWERFUL

How we start doesn't have to dictate how we end. It's all the things that happen in between, the moments where we choose to do the right thing and be better people. We can mend or break a person just by the things we say. You decide the experience others will have with you. How you make them feel is up to you. When you use words, think of the aim. What are you trying to do? Is your intention to cripple them emotionally, embarrass them, create an enemy, make peace, restore faith, or show kindness?

So much of the hurt we experience happens through the use of words. It takes the same amount of energy to congratulate or compliment someone as it does to criticize them. In an instant, you can damage a person's reputation, crush their confidence, open old wounds, or push them over the edge of their personal cliff. Choose to use your speech as an instrument of love, compassion, and understanding. If you can't say something nice, say nothing at all. If it bothers you so much that you must say something negative, write it down. At least you'll get it out of your head. We won't combust if we hold our tongues and choose not to put others down or speak negative manifestations over them. We all have trash in our heads to filter out each day. It's like taking out the garbage. Even the body has its own disposal system. We must get rid of the toxic stuff that can poison us from within. I'm not encouraging you to keep things bottled up. Let it all out, but do so without piling on others just to hurt them. What kind of person throws their garbage onto their neighbor's or their friend's property? Who takes a crap on a stranger or the person they love? At the end of each day, take some time to reflect, pray, meditate, vent out loud, or get a journal and write it all down. Dump it all from your heart and mind, and make room for positive feelings and energy to flow back in. If you don't, then it all just stores up and over time, just like the garbage bin in your home or a backed-up intestine, everything spills over. It makes you sick to your stomach and all the damage caused only leaves you with a big old mess to clean up.

Take back the power of your words and start using them in kindness today. Empty yourself of the negative and poisonous thoughts. Tell people how you feel, but do it in a way that creates understanding, compassion, and resolution, not arguments and confusion. We all know how we would like others to deal with us: directly, respectfully, calmly, and with kindness. Give what you hope to receive. Uplift someone, compliment someone, tell someone you appreciate them. Even when others make it difficult to do so, dig deep and find something that reminds you they are human and that we all make mistakes. Don't expect perfection from others when you're not perfect. Stop using people as your personal punching bags. Use your words to apologize, to resolve conflicts, and to restore broken trust and confidence. Choose to let go of the words that have hurt you. They have no power over you. They don't define you, because every day is another chance to prove that what was said in the past is wrong. We can do this. It will require unlearning some things and learning some new ones, but most of all it will require effort every single day.

When women dislike you because others do like you, whether it's because of a gift you possess, something you've achieved, the way you look, or just the gift of being yourself, they know that you are not the genuine issue. That person is dealing with their own insecurities. Still, having a bright light around you doesn't mean you should cast a shadow over others. No one is beneath you and you are beneath no one. Don't allow the treatment from others to turn you into that which you are not. Don't match people's meanness and poor attitudes. Remember that these women may only know one side of you. Show them what you want them to see. We spend a lot of time complaining about people not knowing us or giving us a chance, but how often are you showing them who you are? How often are you letting your guard down and allowing them to see you? Sometimes the person that you think dislikes you needs a chance as well. Be considerate, especially when you are in a position of favor. Allow others an opportunity to shine. Never take more than you need or have earned, and don't steal opportunities from others just because you can. Don't encourage favoritism; speak up when you see bias and discrimination.

Communication doesn't have to be a scary or complex thing. You don't need to make everyone your best friend, but don't be content making an enemy where there wasn't one. Stop hating people for things outside of their control, like their appearance or their God-given talents. Don't dislike someone because of the attention they receive from others. Don't begrudge someone an accomplishment that you wanted to get to first. It doesn't matter who you are - the woman who hurts others or the one who is hurting. We all feel justified in our reasons, but we can no longer afford to hang on to those excuses. Look that woman in the face, the one that's always with you, always looking at you with an opinion. She's your reflection. Tell her that no matter what happened in her past, she is beautiful, she is strong, and she survived. Tell her she can never control the actions of others, but she can choose how much she allows their choices to hold her back. There's no need to feel ashamed once you've admitted to how you've been treating others or how they have treated you.

Another woman's success, attention, or abilities don't diminish the glory of who you are. You shine differently, but just as brightly. The sky is vast enough, the ocean wide enough, and the earth large enough to host all the greatness in each and every one of us. There is no shortage of space for us to shine. Be happy for another woman's success; you may only be seeing the result or highlights of her hard work without ever knowing how much of a struggle it actually was.

FOUR
BIRTH OF A RESENTMENT

I WAS 16 YEARS OLD WHEN I FAINTED ON MY WAY TO SCHOOL ONE morning and had to be rushed to the hospital. It was there that I first heard the words "anemia" and "seizure." Truth be told, I was never one to starve myself. I've always had a healthy relationship with food, even though my godmother used to spank me to eat vegetables. What kid liked veggies, though? It disturbed both me and my mom when the first rumor around my fall was that I had an eating disorder. It was laughable to those who actually knew me. If anyone could have predicted what would come next, I would have embraced the eating disorder rumor.

Upon returning to school, I had to deal with two of my teachers. You know the ones - they try too hard to be cool and down with the students. Mr. Jose was that teacher—a big burly guy who breathed like a worn-out gorilla and carried the stench of sweat and overpriced cologne. He gossiped with students and was very inappropriate with some of us. I thought he was a creep. Ms. Wells accompanied him. She was bullied in school for being a tomboy and used our high school as her own personal arena for payback. I particularly knew her for picking on students; they were usually attractive and popular, but it's possible that was just a coincidence.

In a class setting, Mr. Jose, in an obnoxious, insensitive, and self-assured way, blurted out, "I heard you were in the hospital because you were pregnant."

The awkward silence was deafening. I looked over at Ms. Wells, expecting some kind of solace. I hoped she would say something to defend or comfort me. At the very least, I wanted her to call out this most inappropriate act from another teacher. Instead, she stood there nodding her head as she ran her pencil eraser across the desk—a devious, smug grin on her face.

It was as if I had entered a horror movie scene where you look up with relief at the person you think will rescue you, only to realize that they've been working with the bad guy all along. At that point, you know that shit's about to get much worse for you. What the hell was happening? School should be a safe space. Teachers should protect their students.

Much outside of my character, I confronted this teacher right there and then. The notion was ridiculous, although very serious. It was damaging, considering that I was still very much a virgin. I could have kicked him in the nuts, but my mom taught me not to be violent.

"What's the matter with you? What are you talking about, Mr. Jose?"

Pacing back and forth and rubbing his hand over his sweaty forehead, he remarked that my best friend was the one behind the rumor. "Why, how could she say something like that!?" My best friend was just as talented as I was. She was intelligent, pretty, and she came from a wealthy family. She had so much more than I did, and my reputation for not hooking up with boys was something that I took great pride in. I didn't judge anybody else or their choices, but I had made a choice a long time ago not to give away my virtue in high school. She knew this, so I didn't understand. I was just hurt and confused.

Ms. Wells just stood there and allowed him to humiliate a student with his vile outburst. The murmurs, snickering, and vilifying stares ensued. Humiliation intensified, and the story grew more elaborate with each telling. The next few days felt longer than usual. On the fourth day, I rushed home during lunch period and the weight of all the things being said about me began choking me. I wore them like a barbed wire chained around my neck, and with every new rumor, I felt it tightening a little more. I had never experienced a full-blown anxiety attack before then.

I began experiencing the loudest and most vivid flashbacks of the past few weeks and drifted into the bathroom. Then, frantic and emotional, I swallowed what was left in two different pill bottles. I needed an end to what I was feeling, and I didn't care what it took. The suffocation needed to stop. I had to shut up the toxic voices in my head, replaying these negative things.

I was fortunate. My mom scrambled to the hospital, and they stammered that I was going to be okay, that I was anemic and suffering from anxiety. I knew instantly that I had to keep it to myself. My attempt to relieve myself of my suffering garnered me no sympathy; it only added fuel to the fire. The rumor now was that I tried to end my own life because I was forced to keep a baby I never carried.

It's a simple thing to ask how anyone could ever try hurting themselves. People criticize that a person who commits suicide only wanted attention. I often wonder, "How stupid can you be? How can a dead person experience attention? They're dead."

God kept me alive that day. I was numb, no longer crying for help, and hoping that it would stop. I was tired of crying and done hoping. These women weren't going anywhere and I couldn't take it anymore.

My mother didn't know how to deal with this. She didn't know who to trust at this stage either, so she decided we couldn't trust anyone. She tried to keep me away from friends and encouraged me to leave the band. For the first time, she even began looking into my options for college away from home—an option she didn't want to consider before. She always said she wanted me close to home. Now an opportunity arose to go to Canada, but I wasn't ready to leave my mom and brothers.

WHEN IT'S HOME THAT'S DESTROYING YOU

It would take a showdown with an older female cousin I used to admire to solidify my increasing resentment toward women. It provided me with that final boost I needed to want to get the hell out of there. She was speaking down to my mother, her own aunt. She was empty of shame and dripping with utter disrespect.

She was hollering at my mom, "You so dumb, you can't read, that's why you child father used to bang you!"

I snarled back at her, "For whatever you think my mother can't do, she'll never have to ask you to do it for her. Her kids will read what she can't, we'll teach her what she doesn't know, and we'll be damned if another soul ever tries to lay a hand on her!"

"Sis, she can say what she wants, as long as she doesn't touch me mudda." It was my brother's stern voice piercing through the dry air from a nearby corner of the room.

With the devil in her eyes and his whip as her tongue, she pivoted toward me and squalled, "I can't stand you! You ain't special and nobody likes you. You face just hard like you mudda. Don't know why people don't stop pitying you. If you never did win dem shows nobody would care 'bout you. You own father don't care 'bout you, no wonder you try kill yous" ef."

The tears no longer flow from my eyes as they did then. The scorched and shattered look on my mother's face was haunting. My nose flared, my eyes widened, and I could feel the bulging veins along my forehead pulsing. I wanted to lunge at her and break her jaw with a slap that would drive her tongue to the back of her throat, then watch her foam at the mouth while she choked on it. Instead, I felt paralyzed and split open.

I only projected a few last words, "You're a hateful, jealous bitch and I can't stand you either. I can't wait to get out of here!"

I decided if girls didn't like me, I didn't like them either. I was ready to leave the fishbowl that almost drowned me. They took the passion and the light from me. I was still a child, and they tried to break me. I had been hurt enough, and if I was ever to feel whole again, I needed to leave. This was the thinking of a teenage girl.

Women couldn't be trusted in my eyes. The more I let them in, the more they used my vulnerabilities against me. The more secrets I revealed, the less they concealed. The more I made myself available for them, the less they showed up for me. The more I defended them to others, the more they talked behind my back.

The more I reached out to them for help, the more helpless they made me feel. I wanted nothing to do with them. I was left questioning everything and everyone, even my own self-worth. Did anyone really care?

ACCEPTANCE AND ACCOUNTABILITY

There is always someone who loves you. However, don't expect that the love they have for you will erase the fact that they are human and will inevitably make mistakes. Just because they anger you, hurt you, or disappoint you at some point doesn't mean that they don't love you or that there is something wrong with you.

For so long I envied other women because they knew who they were and where they belonged. I wondered how they were so content and happy when I was carrying so much darkness inside. No matter where I was, I felt like I didn't belong. I blamed everyone else, until the question was thrown at me: "Why do you feel like this in every situation?" I was forced to face that deep, toxic, terrified place in my mind. It was the place where I would go whenever something bad happened or something didn't work out for me. My thoughts would run off to the most negative places. Thoughts of being unloved, abandoned, a burden, insufficient, incapable, and destined to be alone.

Is that truly how everyone felt about me, or was that just how I felt about myself?

I have a family that loves me, a man who wants the privilege of loving me, and friends who have seen the worst and still choose me. For so long I was battling with my own thoughts. I could tell everyone else how amazing and appreciated they were, but I couldn't say that to myself.

I didn't feel like I deserved it; I didn't feel like I had done anything worthy of it. It never occurred to me that all I needed to achieve was being myself. Love doesn't require us to climb a mountain, make the most money, or look the prettiest. It doesn't require us to impress anyone in order to receive it. It only requires that we are willing and open to accept it when it is given. Receiving love for who we are is the ultimate achievement.

I was holding on to my past, and it was anchoring me to a single state of mind. I had to learn to let go and allow myself to live, change, and move on. We all do. We are all capable of living the life we want, the way we want to live it. I knew my brokenness and I felt weak, ugly, unaccomplished, and not enough because of it. My emotions were hijacked by these negative thoughts that controlled me. That's who I felt I was, but it's not who I wanted to be. How could I feel like I belonged anywhere when I didn't even feel like I belonged to myself?

This competition isn't always as obvious as beauty pageants. Sometimes it's dangerous and covert. Certain women will befriend you, only to learn your secrets and build an arsenal to tear you down because of petty jealousies and insecurities. She will plant seeds of doubt in your head about your friends, family, relationship, or career. This type of woman will encourage you to engage in conflicts instead of resolving them calmly and respectfully. She will insert herself wherever she can and try to destabilize your life from within, while pretending to offer love and support. She will add fuel to rumors instead of putting them out and she won't have much good to say behind your back. Some women will go to extremes to dismantle another woman's life. She'll assassinate your character and reputation, then take away what is dearest—family and friends. Friends will become resentful of other friends for trying to improve their own lives; they will stereotype other women based on social class, culture, color, and faith, and blame other women for things that men have done to hurt them.

Now you might say, "I'm nothing like that." You could be the friend who questions why great things are happening for your best friend and not you, the mom harboring negative feelings toward her friend who has time to do nice things for herself, the woman who has to pretend that she's happy about her crush marrying another woman. Or you could be on the other side of it all: a teacher in a classroom who's a little more creative and unconventional in your methods, a police officer who all the officers respect as their equal, a dancer at a club working your way through college, or a doctor saving other people's lives. At some point, you have been on either side. You have been the woman who compares or talks trash about other women, or you have been the woman who other women have compared themselves to and trash talked. Before you categorize yourself and think about where you want to place other women, be honest with yourself. Change and growth won't happen without honest acceptance and accountability.

SOMETIMES WE DON'T NEED TO RUN

Things will happen in our lives that force us to run away from our problems. If we're honest with ourselves, we'll realize that sometimes it's not because a decision is best for us; sometimes it's just easier. There's nothing wrong with walking away from the things that hurt you. If you don't face the problem and deal with it, it gets packed up with everything else and sooner or later, it unloads itself into your life.

Sometimes the people we love most will be the ones who hurt us most. Your peace of mind is worth removing yourself from anything or anyone toxic. However, in order to find peace ahead, we have to make peace with what we've left behind, especially regarding those close to us. Let that person in your life know that they are hurting you. "I know you care about me but it hurts my feelings when you…" or "I love you, but it makes me feel bad when you…" Give them the opportunity to recognize what they are doing wrong and try to fix it. If it matters to them, they will.

Sometimes people don't even understand why they are being mean to you. They may be angry, hurt, neglected, insecure, or scared themselves. They may never have been taught how to express their emotions without making someone else feel worse. I asked myself so many times, but I never asked them: why? "Why are you treating me this way, what have I done to you?" You'll find that you don't actually have to do anything to a person for them to dislike you, envy you, or hate you. In those cases, at least you know you are not the issue. In other cases, you may uncover things about that person that help you better understand their behavior and attitude toward you.

Why should you care to understand their reasons? You may be the first person to ever do so, or to show them compassion. They may cry out for help to carry the weight of something they've been keeping a secret. They could also reveal something that you did without considering their feelings. An opportunity to help that person heal or see the good within themself could emerge, as well as a chance for you to reflect on what you may have done to contribute to it and make things right. You and you alone might not inspire change in a person, but understanding someone even if we have to distance ourselves from them changes the way we move forward in treating others. When we carry hurt, pain, and anger, sometimes it unleashes itself in similar ways to how it was unleashed on us.

Our issues take time to develop, so allow yourself time to change. If you don't like who you are, change who you are. It really is that simple. The process will take you through some uncomfortable places at times, but when you get there, face it head on. You will laugh, cry, and want to give up sometimes, but keep your focus on reaching the end. Sometimes there are no corners to take, no shortcuts, and no way around. Sometimes going through it is the only way out. Make the choice to be happy and begin your journey.

Don't obsess over what everyone else thinks of you, but for those close to you, ask why. Your friendships and relationships are worth it. So, before you decide to return the favor of hate for hate, before you decide to run away and never look back, ask why. "I'm asking because I care, and I really don't want things to be this way." Your reason for asking might also make a difference to them.

A NEW BEGINNING AND A FINAL FAREWELL

After moving to Canada, I felt an overwhelming urge to establish a better relationship with my father. I needed that fatherly presence and advisor in my life, so I reached out to him, and we began communicating regularly. A year later, he took ill and his health began to deteriorate, although he tried to hide it up until his final few months. It was January 2016, and I decided to write him a letter so he could have something tangible from me. I wrote that letter, placed it in an envelope and sat it down for a couple of days. I thought I had time to mail it out. My father passed away a few days later at the age of 56, and on the eve of my 21st birthday, his body was laid to rest. I wasn't just fractured; I was completely broken. It crippled me, just as I had embarked on becoming a woman - a woman working to make her father proud.

RECOVERY

I never asked my father why he decided to leave me with my mother and take my brother. Somehow, I felt like I already knew. To be honest, I knew he felt like he was only doing what was best for me. In some ways, he did. Could he have been more present in my life? Definitely. Could he have supported my mom and I better? I don't know. What I do know is that my father loved me. He said he didn't know how to make his way back into my life after missing so much of it. Well, what do you know? Even adults can feel afraid and embarrassed.

I'll never know if he did his best or not. I'll never know what it feels like to have your father in the front row as you accept an award. I'll never get the opportunity to introduce him to a guy or have him walk me down the aisle. I'll never be able to ask him if he was in fact proud of me. I'll never understand why or how, but I felt his pride in me. I felt his love for me and I felt his regret over not having enough time with me. I can't say I knew who my dad was completely. I can only say that I had one. He was far from perfect; late, yet still right on time. I carry the best parts of him and I forgave the rest. One year just wasn't enough.

Pain was necessary for my self-development. I migrated from the negative thoughts of others and recognized my own self-worth. I chose life. I chose to start living. Even on the worst days, life is worth living. You are loved. Walk toward the pain and keep pushing through it, because on the other side there is beauty. Live to see that amazing place you've never visited. Live to taste that incredible dish you have yet to try. Live to experience that earth shattering kiss that makes your knees go weak and your heart skip a beat. Live to do that thing you thought was impossible.

Before we can do anything else, we must be grateful to be alive, because it is only the living who can love. Only by living can we change the world. We are still here, and it is not a coincidence or an accident. It is easy to hate, easy to fear, easy to distrust and avoid. Love is the hardest thing to do. Yet it is the most powerful tool we have and the only thing strong enough to get this job done. We must survive and live so that we can love and give.

ADMITTING THAT WE NEED EACH OTHER

Throughout my adult life, I have experienced tragedy, pain, and disappointment. I felt like I was unique in my suffering, even though there were women halfway across the world experiencing my same struggles. Across the street there were women who could relate to what I was going through. Sitting right next to me on a bus were women who had been through worse.

When we count others out over our differences, we miss the opportunity to count on each other over our similarities. I've been blessed to be influenced by the positive examples of many women in my life today. I have an amazing support system made up of all types of women from all walks of life. It began with women older than myself who weren't related to me by blood, but they felt like family. These were the women my mother strategically placed in my life at an early age — women I could and would always run back to for advice and guidance no matter how much time had passed or how many mistakes I had made. Sometimes, it's those moments when we look up and see the most unexpected faces, hear the most unexpected voices, and experience the most unexpected kindness. They stand out and change who we are.

At different stages in my life, these women shattered my flawed perception of women. Not all women were catty, untrustworthy, unsupportive, and too much drama. The positive changes in my life were inspired by some of their actions. They led me here to this very place at this very moment writing this book.

They helped shape the woman that I am. I no longer pretend that I'm better off without companionship or friends. We want to have people we can trust and depend on. There is independence in being able to admit that we depend on the love and support of the women in our lives. I could no longer convince myself that my dislike for other women was normal or acceptable, when the truth was that I wanted to be welcomed, accepted, and appreciated by them.

Now to you, that might make me sound needy, soft, or even pathetic. I chose to stop hiding behind words like, "I'm an introvert, that's why I keep to myself," or, "I only hang out with guys because girls are too much drama," or even, "I'm an independent woman who doesn't need anything from anyone." That wasn't gonna cut it for me anymore. We don't have to be alone to be independent.

I don't know about you, but I wouldn't want to exist by myself. I wouldn't want to exist without friendships. I wouldn't want to exist without love. Everything's better with family and friends. Food is more enjoyable, vacations are more fun, even crying feels better with friends. There was nothing to brag about by not having anyone I could trust and who could trust me. There was nothing glamorous about being all dressed up in a room filled with other people, but having no real connection with anyone. There was nothing fun or cute about having successes in life and no one to share them with. There was nothing to laugh about while braving through hardships alone.

For all the contacts in my telephone, there was no one I felt I could trust enough to confide in. There was nothing lonelier than experiencing things only a woman would understand, but having no women to share those things with.

We can have it all in the material world: money, fame, success, beautiful things, and a wonderful relationship. Still, none of that can compensate for the value of true friendship and sisterhood.

A DIFFERENT ATTITUDE

By my own account, I was flailing after my dad died. My faith was shaken. I was lapsing on my student loan payments. I felt like I was failing my mom and my entire family back in the Caribbean. I felt entirely purposeless and my self-esteem had plummeted. I decided to do what any sane person would do: I got a job. I started waitressing at a delightful Italian restaurant. When I first applied, I had no experience. What I did have was a good personality and an eagerness to learn—out of sheer desperation to improve my circumstances, of course.

You know that woman who walks into a room with effortless beauty? Like she didn't even brush her hair or put on makeup, but you still see her? That was Mae. She was subtle, but self-assured and confident. She was experienced, and I knew it the first day we worked together. She could also be impatient when it came to tasks that she considered simple.

"It's not rocket science, girl," she would sometimes mutter with a smile.

It was like being in a pageant all over again. Only this time, all the other contestants were much more prepared and experienced than I was. There were plenty of blundering moments that kept me apologizing. I'd mess up and call myself an idiot under my breath for making a mistake.

Mae would always say, "No hun, you're not an idiot, you're still learning. Wait and see, you're gonna master this stuff."

When Mae spoke, you believed her. She still has that effect today. She spoke to me as if she had a crystal ball that showed her all the things I would be able to do. There was seldom a time when she said I would get good at something, and I didn't do just that.

She didn't know how much I was struggling with grief when we met. Having no family in Canada, I relied on the validation of my partner, as if he was life support and I'd die without it. It didn't take her long to bulldoze the wall I had put up. We became fast friends, bonding over food, our desire to do something that makes the world a better place, and oh yes, food. She was a culinary graduate and I knew my way around the kitchen. After observing my relationship first hand, Mae was convinced that I deserved better. It was clear that the efforts I was putting in weren't being reciprocated. She wasn't shy about voicing it either.

A few of the other girls devised a plan to divide and conquer after realizing how close Mae and I had gotten. They would make comments claiming that Mae had complained about something I had done, then go back and do the same thing with her. There was nothing amusing about it. If only I'd had the maturity I have now . I still can't believe how easy it was (and still is) in today's society for women to plant seeds of doubt in another woman's head by identifying a weakness.

They saw that Mae was more like a teacher to me with work and managed to prey on my insecurity. I began comparing myself to my new friend.

"How come she's so strong and I'm not?"

"She's so comfortable being herself around everyone."

"She's so much better at this job than I am."

Once you start comparing yourself to others, jealousy isn't too far behind. There was something different about this situation though. I wasn't dealing with the same breed of woman here at all. She wasn't going to be bamboozled and she wasn't going to allow me to be swept up in it.

The other girls didn't encourage a lot of collaboration. They would bicker with the manager over who worked when and try to undercut me. Some days, they made sure I got the smallest number of shifts to work, claiming seniority. If it wasn't for Mae, I'd never have been able to get a shift covered if I'd needed to miss work.

One of the women even threatened to contact immigration after she accused me of sneaking my way into the country. She didn't even bother asking what my status in the country was. All she knew was that I had an accent, so I must have snuck into the country somehow. Another one would joke and ask how the trip across the ocean was in the box on the boat I had supposedly arrived in. I'd usually laugh it off and say, "As comfortable as you can imagine a can of sardines to be." I'm not very pugnacious, so I chose my battles with caution. Most times I ignored the obtuse commentary about my origins.

There was never any team work while working with the other girls. It was every woman for herself. The nights would often end in puerile arguments over who did what, why this one deserves more of the gratuity than the other, or how someone was being too friendly with regulars. Mae took me under her wing, kept me close, and always defended me. She also pretended not to notice my little jealousies toward her. She began working a few parties with me and we soon became a dynamic duo. We were so cohesive. One night while working, she caught me in the back crying. She marched into the kitchen demanding to know who did what to me and whose ass needed to be kicked. Later that same night as we counted out our tips together, she expressed how the other girls didn't understand that when we work together, it's way less stressful. Things run more smoothly .

A BREAKTHROUGH

After going through a terrible breakup, Mae had begun smoking and drinking again. My friend, who was so strong, was fighting a battle I couldn't relate to. The only thing I knew how to do was be present. I showed up for her everyday whether she wanted me to or not. We worked on it together. She refocused her energy into catering — something she loved and had wanted to do for a very long time. I didn't know at the time that there was a deeper cause for her pain. It became clear to me that she and I were more alike than I had thought.

Her biological dad was not in the picture and she had a complicated relationship with her mom and stepdad, even though she loved them to death. She was hurting so much and I didn't know how to break through. How could I? I hadn't broken through my own pain.

Swept up in emotion, I broke down and shared my story with her. It was heartbreaking and I could feel the emotion like heavy chunks making their way down my throat. It was the first time since my father had passed away that I felt comfortable opening up to another female, or any other person for that matter.

47

Up until that moment I had never openly acknowledged the source of my pain and resentments. I hadn't let it go, even though I got my dad back for a short time. Right then, Mae began talking. We talked for hours. I couldn't believe how confident and strong we both were at that moment. Charged with emotion, all we could do was embrace each other. It became calm for a moment as we began drawing away.

That's when she said, "I still have time to make amends, but there are things that you never asked your father, things that you never said and confrontations that you never had. The unanswered questions still tear you apart. The regret of never asking and not knowing is eating you up inside."

She was right. I blamed myself. How could I ever believe that my father didn't reject me, if he never actually told me so? I never got confirmation that it wasn't my fault and I didn't know how to live with that.

"You were a child and your parents loved you very much. They just didn't love each other as much anymore. It wasn't your fault, hun. Let it go," she said. "Just let it go."

My father was gone; there would be no more conversations, no opportunity to ask one more question, say one more thing, or create one new memory.

I know what you may be thinking. Why didn't I ask all those questions while he was alive? The answer is simple. I thought we would have time. I didn't want to spend a moment trying to get back my lost time, because I was happy creating new memories in the present. My father was gone and the only way to move forward was to let it all go.

I thought about the last year of his life and all the love I felt from him. It had to be enough, because there was no more time. Suddenly, it was. I knew that my father may not have had all the right answers, even if he was still alive. All I knew and cared about was that he loved me and was happy to be in my life again. There are things that need to be said to be believed; then there are those things that need to be felt to be believed. I got the chance to experience my father's love. I felt it and that's all that mattered.

"Daddy, you caused me so much pain and I'll never truly understand why, but with every heartbeat inside of me, I forgive you." It needed to be said out loud. "It hurts, oh God, it hurts so much!" I screamed as I felt the words coursing through my veins like fire and ice. I don't know how I ended up on my knees. It was as though my knees gave out and my entire body became weak and numb. All that hurt, anger, resentment, and regret over my father departed from me. I had to make the choice to let it go, to focus on the good, and to allow one single fact to override all others. My father was imperfect and he loved me as much as I loved him.

In helping my friend, I was forced to split myself open and confront my own issues — issues I thought I had come to terms with. Until I said it all out loud, it was still my secret burden and emotional handicap to bear. There, in the most vulnerable state that I had ever seen her, Mae managed to reassure me that everything was going to be alright and things would get better; all we had to do was choose it. We had to choose to be better and do better than the people and circumstances that hurt us.

She said, "I'm so happy we met."

So was I. For the first time, Canada began to feel like a home. I felt safe, and now I had family there.

TRANSCENDING FRIENDSHIP

There was something to be admired about her. I had not yet reached that point in my growth — the ability to care for a friend as I cared for my own sister, and having the desire to protect and defend them. I realized that everything she had shown me, everything she had ever said to me, was genuine. We came from different places. We were of different skin colors, religions, and cultures, yet our values were not that different. Our dreams and desires to do good in the world and to be good and happy people were not different. Our differences didn't separate us; they were the very things that made us complement each other so well.

She has never needed to prove herself. She taught me how to trust a friend by being a trustworthy one. She taught me how to cheer for a friend by always cheering me on. She taught me by showing me every day that she wanted the same greatness for me as she wanted for herself. That was a feeling I was familiar with, but not from a friend. It was something I had only felt from my mother and my siblings back home. I discerned that if another woman loved and cared about me as much as my family did, then that made her family to me. Throughout the years, Mae superseded being a friend and became my sister. Cooking together, going through breakups, hardships, living, laughing, and learning from each other — this is the friendship that nurtured me.

We should all try to nurture the friendships we have — water them daily with words and actions of love and sincerity and watch them blossom. We can dismantle the pretenses and begin getting to the root of these issues; we can assess ourselves, how we fit into this problem, and accept responsibility. From there, we can start to change the habits that got us here — to lead a new frontier of women toward a dynamic of sisterhood instead of competitors.

We can't be cavalier about the impact on us and young girls. They are comparing themselves when they should be embracing their individuality. We can no longer proceed with the attitude of, "I don't live there, so that problem doesn't affect me," or, "That's not my daughter, so it's not my problem," or, "I don't know you so I don't care." The detrimental effect this approach has had and will continue to have on women may be catastrophic. It would be a tragedy not to afford this new generation of women the opportunity to arm themselves. We must all strive to be better examples, not to mention the domino effect that this has on our health, on our households, and on our societies and cultures. We are the fabric of our societies, the fortifiers of our families and our communities. It has always been us. The only way to change the condition of how we treat others is to change the condition within our own hearts.

FIVE
THE GRATIFICATION OF SELF-PROMOTION

"Women are too dramatic and judgmental, that's why all my friends are men."

How often have we heard this transparent declaration? It only feeds an indulgence for self-gratification when we criticize someone else while propping ourselves up. It is a false and fleeting sense of fulfillment when we feel the satisfaction of somehow being better than another person. When I discovered how often women turned on each other in the presence of men, then had the audacity to say, "This is why I don't deal with females and I vibe with guys more," I deduced that there had to be an unspoken motivation for this type of behavior.

One reason for this attitude is the attention and affection of men. Men are that vital piece of the puzzle which many women feel can provide that picture perfect life, a life complete with children, a career, a home, and stability. Let's face it — most women will never admit that this way of operating has anything to do with earning the attention of men.

Women have been competing with other women over men for centuries. Sometimes, women are even groomed in the "art" of seducing a man and stealing him from another. For some women, men are the missing piece to their picture of happiness; if he is doing right by another woman, meaning he treats her like a princess, he provides for her, protects and respects her, there are some women who aim to have him for themselves. He is being too good to his woman, and she seems to have the life and happiness that you want. This is because we often attach happiness to things or a person. Here, it's that man. You presume that her state of happiness has more to do with him, and you want that (him) for yourself. If he makes her that happy, then he will make you happy, too.

To snag that reward (the man), the woman herself must appear as a worthy prize in his eyes — and as a prize sought after by other men. Most women have a need to be desired by men, and to be seen as the most desirable option among other women. Some women have an insatiable desire to always have the attention of men. Even after they have settled down with someone, they need to know that other men find them attractive and desirable.

There is nothing twisted about wanting the attention of a man. However, when this aspiration undermines all moral reasoning and decency, when it becomes borderline to fully obsessive, that needs to be noticed. The efforts to maintain that attention can be disastrous; sometimes, it can even be fatal. You put yourself in that man's direct view every chance you get. You fish for compliments and feel invalidated and resentful when you don't receive them. You find everything wrong with that other woman, even though she has done you no wrong.

We will investigate another woman all because a man is interested in her or finds her appealing. Some women will spend hours combing the internet and social media, hoping to find fault with that woman. Some will rifle through every photo of her and start comparing themselves, dredging up any reason to say something negative about her. This type of behavior has got to stop. It's unhealthy and time-consuming. There are so many useful ways to better spend our time.

We are usually aware of the physical qualities that attract the man we are interested in. This causes us to pick apart other women with these attributes, which offers little satisfaction in the long run. Allowing jealousies and bad feelings to poison your soul over women who are younger or more attractive won't make them age any faster or appear any less attractive to the men you're competing for. It is not her fault that she is younger, and it is not your fault that you have passed her age. You are both beautiful and both worthy of love. This is one of the major areas where the female competition has gotten dangerously out of control. Women are dying on tables every day, convinced that their bodies need fixing to be more desirable to men and to compete with other women. There is nothing wrong with wanting to work on the body that you came in if it makes you feel better about yourself, but first examine why you don't feel great about yourself to begin with. You may end up at a much simpler, cheaper, and less risky conclusion.

This jealousy and hate toward other women over men can fester into severe depression as well. Full-blown obsessions and psychological issues can develop. It can become so life-consuming that outside intervention is necessary. There is no man who can make us happy; we have to make ourselves happy. A good spouse can only complement the work that we have already done for ourselves. They can only add to what we have already established within us — that love, joy, happiness, self-worth, peace, and contentment we feel in and about ourselves. We have a duty to make ourselves whole.

Another person cannot create what isn't already within you. We are the masters of our own happiness. It comes from inside. It is not anything or anyone external. If we lay our happiness at the feet of a man, what happens if that man stomps on it, or leaves? There goes our happiness, right along with him. If we allow men or anyone else to validate who we are, we give them the power to invalidate who we are with a simple change of mind or cruel words. Love yourself, want yourself, respect yourself, and understand yourself before anyone else can. Try it!

The other woman might appear happier to you because of her ability to generate her own light. She already shines. The man you attribute her happiness to has only merged his light with hers. The two beam stronger and brighter together. Neither of them compensates for what the other lacks on the inside. The sooner we realize that no one else can carry our light for us, the sooner we can move forward in creating a life we actually love.

IT'S HOW YOU CHOOSE TO LOOK AT THINGS

When we perceive another woman as a threat, we stand in the way of something that she wants and usually feels she deserves. We convey a message to whoever will listen that the other woman is a terrible team player, all to elevate ourselves by making her look bad. You want the promotion, the job, the scholarship, or the role in that movie, and she's standing between you and your dream. You want to control the outcome by manipulating those around you, because you believe you deserve the recognition for something, so you turn others against her and toward your favor. Then there are the ill-wishers, those women who can never celebrate the wins of another woman unless they were a part of it or it benefits them. There is no personal gain in it for them. It's not their achievement, so they find it difficult to be happy for the other woman and go as far as hoping and praying that she fails.

We don't have to be a part of someone's accomplishment to be happy for their success.

A new stage is set, and there are no rules. Fame, financial wealth, beauty, class, and status are only a few segments of the competition. It's like the Hunger Games, but instead of trying to win to feed an entire community, it's about taking each other down to feed egos, vendettas, wants, and temptations. Creating rumors and breaking the confidence of another woman is like a sport to some. They find it thrilling. Why is it so much easier to believe the worst about another woman, but question anything good about her? Well, because no one is actually living the perfect life. No woman actually has it all figured out. Some are simply faking it until they make it, and we're all just making up the rest as we go.

Bringing attention to people's faults shouldn't make us feel better about ourselves. We are all flawed. No one wants to be perceived as the only liar, failure, cheater, backbiter, or insecure one in the room. There are those who get satisfaction in hearing that someone else has done worse than they did. It makes their skeletons appear less dusty. It somehow makes them feel like whatever they may have done, at least wasn't as bad as what she (the other woman) has done. Too often, we are eager to chime in with negative opinions about a woman doing something wrong. All the while, we're doing the same damn thing or worse, but won't admit it. The only concern is for self and image preservation. Well, what about the other woman's image?

Have you ever been out with friends and a stunning woman walks by? She's poised and confident. Without speaking a single word, she commands the attention of everyone in the room. One of your friends comments on her presence. She points out how much that woman craves attention with a haughty interjection. Another goes on about how happy she is to be nothing like that and how much she herself hates attention. Two things happened there. They debased another woman whose only crime was existing, and propped themselves up at the same time. To make themselves look better, she had to look worse. Ask yourself: why?

INVALIDATING BAD BEHAVIOR

When we validate that kind of behavior by our peers or participate in it, we feel an instant sense of empowerment and satisfaction. A false sense of superiority surfaces. It's like telling the guy who's crushing on your friend that you don't think she is his type because she's a little wild. But you don't stop there; you ensure he knows you're the complete opposite, even if you have no genuine interest in him. He compliments you. You act coy, and for the moment, you get an inflated ego. You get a rush of instant gratification and you're pleased with yourself. And for what? Because his interest was in her and not you? Do you dislike her? You don't want to see her happy with anyone, especially if you're not? Whatever the reason, it's never worth it. When we have to steam roll our friends to make ourselves look better or to get ahead, the end never justifies the means.

One day while sitting amongst a few women, a friend stuttered in sadness, "Yeah, I wish my girlfriend could cook."

Tasha, the most brazen of the group, made a malignant comment. "Man, you need to get rid of her." She continued to criticize his girlfriend's ability to be a wonderful mother because she couldn't cook. Tasha proceeded to self-promote by asserting her capabilities in the kitchen, bragging about how she keeps her men by feeding them well.

"How can you be so harsh in your criticism when you're supposed to be friends?" Wait! "Oh shit!" You know that awkward moment when you realize your thoughts slipped out of your mouth? Oops! "Thinking out loud."

This was that moment for my friend Kenna. She held her ground and insisted that she thought Tasha was a friend to the woman she had insulted behind her back.

Her comeback was instant: "I'm just telling it like it is, and I would say it to her face."

Now, usually when a person gets called out for backbiting and employs the line, "I would say it to their face," nine out of ten times, that's some bullshit. They aren't saying a damn thing to that person's face.

There is absolutely nothing wrong with honesty, especially among friends, but you can be honest without being hurtful. It bothered Kenna so much that she later approached Tasha and inquired.

"Tasha, since you're a better cook, why wouldn't you share a few recipes with your friend and teach her how to cook? I'm sure she would appreciate it. She may not have learnt to cook the way you did growing up."

I watched in utter surprise as the arrogance departed from Tasha's attitude. They sat down and Kenna asked her how she would feel if someone reported that Tasha's friend spoke of her in such a critical manner, and what she felt she gained in that moment of backbiting on her friend. Tasha became flushed with embarrassment as she began confiding. She was going through some personal difficulties which everyone was aware of.

Her voice shook and cracked as she proceeded, "I don't know. Things have been rough with me in my personal life."

She was being sincere. I hadn't ever seen her be so transparent.

She placed her elbows on the kitchen countertop, huffed, and lowered her gaze as she spoke. "You know, sometimes when we see other people appearing to have it all when we don't, we leap at the opportunity to magnify their weaknesses to distract from ours."

Her response was jarring. I couldn't believe how candid she was being. Had Kenna attacked her or exposed her misfortunes to prove her point, Tasha would have gotten defensive. She would have learnt no lesson. It was a teachable moment for us all. Sometimes, we just need to hold each other accountable. Sometimes all we need is a mirror held up to our faces long enough for the truth about ourselves to pierce through the masks we wear for the rest of the world. There is no benefit to tearing another woman down that will earn us any long-term blessings. We reap what we sow. It is my belief that often when we stumble across hardships in our lives, it could be because of the ill deeds we have committed against others. When we treat others as we would have them treat us, we pass on hope, trust, and love for humanity.

CHANGE YOUR ROLE

The message girls are receiving is that as women, we can't all be great, beautiful, accepted, worthy, and enough. They learn that there is not enough room for us all to be amazing women, so we have to sacrifice a few women by knocking them down. Children pick up on the way their parents and other grownups discuss one another. We can't continue to talk about each other like adversaries, yet still expect our daughters to be compassionate and understanding toward other girls. They will develop an opinion based on what adults say or feel about other women.

Many of us were fortunate not to have been born in a time of segregation. However, we don't have to look very far to see segregation happening right in front of us. Women have classified each other into groups. Imagine a group of young girls refusing to hang out or eat at a lunch table with other girls, not because of the color of their skin, but because they think those girls are not pretty or popular enough. They don't live on the right side of town. They're not wealthy enough. They're ghetto. On the flip side, they are too bougie, too pretty, or they have too much money. Television shows and social media keep us fixated on the things that should matter the least about people. We know this because we don't ever actually know these people on camera. That world is not real, and unfortunately, we get brainwashed into choosing sides and developing attachments and stereotypes. We misjudge people because of these twisted, made for entertainment moments. The more outrageous the behavior, the more salacious the story, the more people seem to want to watch. We've become so out of touch with reality and the genuine feelings of other women that there is no filter anymore. There seems to be a newfound freedom and validation in saying the cruelest things to and about one another, choosing circles based on social status, wealth, fame, color, geography, and aesthetics. Meanwhile, we put down those we regard as unworthy of being seen with us. The way we detach from other women and put them down, while praising ourselves and men is upsetting, ridiculous and contemptuous.

It makes no sense to continue ignoring the fact that we all contributed to the problem at one point or another. There will always be another woman who is better at something that we also excel at. That does not diminish the fact that we are also great. There is a vast difference between admiration and jealousy. We can learn from someone we admire. We choose not to absorb anything from someone of whom we're jealous. Our prideful deficiencies won't allow us to acknowledge that they may have a positive impact on our life. We all have unique qualities about us. Most times, the women we're comparing ourselves to don't even appeal to the same type of person we would attract to us and vice versa. Believe it or not, we do not attract all men in the same way and a great guy will settle down with the woman he finds peace with, not just beauty. The same career would not make all women happy. Having children wouldn't make all women feel fulfilled, and the same goes for not having any. One size does not fit all. Some of us might find that we would feel out of place and miserable if we traded lives with another woman, even for a day.

We don't always know the things that lie beneath the surface of smiles or perceived happiness. As long as you show up and do your best, that's all that matters.

We allow ridiculous fallacies to dictate feelings about ourselves and each other — such as what we choose to accept and what we won't, and who is worthy of being our friend and who isn't. We create categories and decide which woman goes where, sometimes without ever getting to know her. We could all use more understanding, but we could also offer more understanding to others. While being open-minded is easier said than done, we can do it. We must dig deep and find it within ourselves to stop, look with our hearts, listen, feel, think, and then respond. Then, an incredible change can emerge.

Let's ask ourselves, "How do I want to affect this person? How do I want them to feel about me? Do I want them to leave me better or worse than they came?"

We all have something to offer. None of us are here by accident. No one's purpose is more significant than that of another. Ponder on these questions.

- What if we lived our lives not only in service to ourselves, but in service to each other?
- What if other women cheered for your success?
- What if they helped you when you needed it most? Defended you on life's battlefield and spoke up for you and not against you?
- What if you could start being this kind of woman to other women?
- What if at the same moment, those other women made these exact changes wherever they are?

Now ask yourself, "Wouldn't this be a better reality to live in and a better example for the children?"

It doesn't have to be a bunch of what ifs. We have all the tools to make these changes. Deep down, I know women want to have better relationships with one another. The alternative is a bitter experience, and it doesn't make us feel good about ourselves or each other. To look up and feel that sisterhood surrounding you is what we all have to look forward to. This type of woman is not a myth. She is you, she is me; she is every one of us.

I met Kenna when I was 19 years old in Canada, although we didn't see each other that often during those first couple of years. That all changed once I moved closer to where she and her family were living. We had heaps of fun together. We were both from the same Caribbean Island and she became the only person I trusted to do my hair. The girl's got skills for centuries when it comes to doing hair. When Kenna had her daughter, she asked me to be godmother. I was humbled and in my early twenties with no clue what that entailed. I reluctantly said yes—a decision I'm thrilled that I made. Kenna was a firecracker, let me tell you. She was quick witted, direct, and bold as hell. You especially didn't mess with her family or her friends.

From the beginning, she always came across as the big sister I wished I had grown up with, one who protects you. She would have squared off with some of my cousins back then for sure. Who doesn't love a warrior friend? With all that said, you wouldn't take her for the sensitive type, but she was. She has a huge heart, and is one of the most generous women I know. She was not combative without provocation. Kenna was always there for me. In some ways, she looked out for me and protected me like a mother would. She knew I didn't have family there so she made me a part of hers. I would spend holidays there, weekends, attend parties, you name it. Kenna's home always reminded me of being back in the Caribbean. She was always cooking something, listening to music, or having people over to share in some fun. I was baffled by how some of the women in her life could be so cruel toward her.

Kenna wasn't a college graduate. She had to fend for herself after having her son. She worked hard doing what she could to provide and make a good life for her two kids. One day, she called me almost in tears. She told me that a close friend of hers had said some nasty things behind her back. Still, she entertained this person and had them over at her house during get togethers. This kept happening with different friends over a period of time, yet she would not cut them off.

At a house party Kenna hosted one night, a friend said to her husband, "Your wife just has a pretty face and can cook. When she opens her mouth, she sounds like a dummy who can't speak proper English."

She continued by assuring Kenna's husband that she herself was a college graduate who wouldn't embarrass a man. You can imagine the jaw dropping fury when I visited Kenna a few weeks later to get my hair done and saw that same woman. How could she have spoken about my friend with such vitriol and then gone to hang out in her living room? I couldn't believe it. I actually started questioning if I was being a bad friend by advising Kenna to get far away from that person.

My sentiments were, "Why is she here? Cut her off before she hurts you even worse."

I didn't see it. I didn't see any signs that my friend was suffering internally. When Kenna told me she was sick and needed to undergo major surgery, my heart broke. All I could think about were her two beautiful children. I began spending more time at her house, doing whatever I could to make her comfortable.

At the same time, I was going through a rough patch with my longtime boyfriend. He and I were living together, but the relationship had grown toxic, although neither of us were ready or willing to call it quits. I was looking for any excuse to be away from the house, so going to Kenna's during that time was as much for me as it was for her. There was no escaping what my friend was preparing to face. She showed impeccable strength throughout the entire process.

When she left the hospital, she asked me to come and stay with her during her recovery. She didn't need to ask twice.

Kenna couldn't move around for weeks, couldn't sit up straight, couldn't eat much, walk, or stand for too long. Her son and daughter were like my own niece and nephew. The love and respect there was mutual. She was having a terrible reaction to the mix of medications she was taking. Each day I would sort out her prescriptions and make sure she was taking them on schedule. Some of them only made her feel worse. I can't begin to tell you the depth of despair I felt seeing my friend in such pain. I felt useless because no matter how much I was doing, I couldn't make the agony stop. I would lay next to her at night when her husband would have to work late. One night after carefully helping her from her bed down to the living room, I got her lip gloss and fruity flavored chewing gum which she simply refused to live without. She said everything tasted like metal. We laid on the couch swaddled up under some blankets. We were watching tv and she began unburdening her feelings.

"Girl, you know you're the only friend I could have called to do this for me and to be here for the kids."

I couldn't help but ask about those friends who I knew were not good to her. Her face was dewy and kind, but her eyes were fatigued.

Saddened, she said, "At any moment we could be taken from this world. Even though those women weren't good friends toward me, I remain kind to them. Not because they did anything to deserve it, but because I know who I want to be and how I want to be remembered."

She went on to say that sometimes they would call or text and apologize. And the moment someone apologized, she gave them a clean slate to start over, no matter how many times it happened.

"Who are we to place a number on how many times a person deserves forgiveness, when we ourselves have countless things to be forgiven for?"

It was a profound question and I couldn't answer her. I have always respected Kenna, but my respect for her doubled in that moment.

During that conversation she told me that if her situation ever got worse and she died, I needed to take care of her kids.

"You need to marry my husband," she said. "There's no one I would trust more to care for my family."

Nervous that she would see right through the terrified look on my face, I laughed. I could feel my rear teeth grinding because I didn't know what else to do at that moment. I held her hand and told her, "You're not going anywhere and no one could, or was about to replace you in this family. Least of all me."

She mentioned it two more times during her recovery and each time it was met with a similar response from me. I couldn't imagine losing my friend like that. Her family needed her. I needed her.

Her mom came to visit about a month later and we bonded like mother and daughter. She told me that Kenna and I operated more like sisters than friends. Kenna recovered after some months had passed. My warrior princess has been fighting the good fight every day since then. It hasn't been easy, but she's a fighter and one of the strongest women I am blessed to know.

It wasn't at all clear to me back then, but I was beginning to realize a theme was developing. The word "friend" seemed to have become somewhat of a framed art piece with an ambiguous feel. It was all about how each individual interpreted it. What was certain was that the characteristics of my new friendships had evolved. It was something much more powerful and binding: a sisterhood. This is the friendship that humbled me.

WE ARE ALL QUEENS

What do we gain by putting other women down while promoting ourselves? The real answer is nothing. The satisfaction you've achieved by tearing someone else down is not winning at all — it's nothingness. It's an empty space you're attempting to fill through superficial means. The result you think you've obtained is an illusion.

We don't all have to get to the top at the same time, and we don't need to run over each other to get there. Working together can often get us there much faster. If it so happens that you get there first, don't kick rocks down at those below you. Extend a hand or a road map instead.

Satisfaction comes from knowing you've done your best with integrity and fairness. Gratitude comes from being happy with whatever the outcome may be because you tried. It comes from being content with what you have instead of focusing on what you don't, and from remembering that things could always be worse.

Whether the guy chooses you or not, whether you get the promotion or not, whether your child is the top student in class or not, whether you have three degrees or none, just be happy knowing that you are living a life where you do your best. Give 100% each day to everything because you are living a life that is worthwhile. Your best and her best may not be the same, but she cannot be you better than you can be, like you can't be her better than she can be. Your light brightens a darkness in life that no one else's can in quite the same way.

It is impossible for jealousy and hate to exist and thrive where gratitude lives. Be grateful that you are here, that you can still make a difference. Appreciate all the love, laughter, and joy in your life — all the things that money can't buy.

Another woman shining does not put out your spark. The sun is a star as well, but it doesn't compete with the other stars at night. We each have a purpose, a time, and a place designated for us to shine. All you have to do is your very best. When it's your time, no pretty face, no rumor, and no schemes or plots will be able to take that moment from you. When we try to take those moments from other women, we not only cheat them; we end up cheating ourselves in the long run, since that blessing may not have been meant for us even though we wanted it. That guy might not have been the right guy for you even though you wanted him at the time. The promotion might have taken you away from your family for too long. What is meant for you already has your name written all over it. All you have to do is work hard, be kind, have faith, and be patient.

Allow people to see who you are without having to self-promote by putting down others. Just because that's who you were yesterday, doesn't mean that's who you have to be today. Get genuinely excited for other women doing well. I love telling other people about how amazing the women in my life are, and how great they are at what they do. It doesn't matter if one is a painter and the other one sells paint or if one of them is rich and one isn't. It's the value people bring in their character, not their bank accounts, that matters most. Lend yourself to another woman's team. You never know if you may be the only person she has in her corner rooting for her. That can make a world of difference in someone's life.

We are all queens and the rest of the world is hell bent on shifting our crowns. Let's adjust them for each other.

SIX
IT'S NOT ALL YOUR FAULT

WORKING HARD TO ACHIEVE YOUR GOALS, EXCEEDING EXPECTATIONS, breaking records, or getting that promotion are nothing to feel bad about. It bothers me to see women downplay their achievements, their intellect, and their personality in the presence of other women and even men so they don't appear to be flaunting their successes. I've also known women who enjoyed a good competition and the rush of winning without demeaning someone else. In these cases, the agenda is not to degrade other women or make them feel less than. They are not looking to prove that they are better than the other woman.

We have become a very reactive society. A woman talking about how great her job, her home, or her family are doesn't mean that she is putting yours down. Consider the fact that these may just be areas of her life that she is proud of and grateful for. For all you know, they may be the only things going right in her life. Do not be so quick to judge. Be eager and willing to give other women the benefit of the doubt. It is what we would want for ourselves.

On the other end of the spectrum, there are women who take every win and use it to make other women feel inferior to them, gloating in ways that suggest, "I'm better than you," or, "I have this and I've accomplished that. What have you done?" This type of woman makes other women feel incapable, lazy, weak, and unaccomplished. The worst part is that's the intent.

This desire to prove that we are the ideal woman, that we are every woman wrapped in one, is exhausting. We create standards that even we sometimes fall short of, yet we're firm in holding other women to them. We magnify their shortcomings and label their way of living as incorrect all because they don't do things the same way we do. Don't prey on or mock the insecurities of others. We all have insecurities and we all have things we are afraid of. We must open our hearts and not be so narrow-minded.

There's no wrongdoing in celebrating our wins. I encourage it. Hard work and dedication deserve recognition. Still, we must use not only our heads but our hearts as well. Discerning how to navigate certain situations is key. If your personal relationship is going great and you're talking to someone whose relationship isn't, it may be best to exhibit some tact before going on and on about how wonderful your relationship is to that person. There will be other opportunities to do that.

Sometimes we need to assess what's most important and most appropriate in the present. You shouldn't have to hide your promotion because your friend got fired. You are not the only one in this situation; your friend also has a choice to make. Should she congratulate you and be happy for you, or should she resent you and make you feel bad for still having a job?

I can recall a situation where a friend and I had good news to celebrate. Our mutual friend had some terrible news to share. We all met up one evening and exchanged our news. My friend and I decided that we would have plenty of time to celebrate later, even though our mutual friend insisted we celebrate in spite of her news. At that moment, we made a choice to be the support that she needed. We spent the evening reminding her of how talented she was and reassured her that better was in store for her. The way we thought about it, being available for her and putting off the celebration of our win took nothing away from us. Being there for our friend gave something back to her after she had lost something that mattered. It didn't change the fact that we had something to celebrate. When the time came, she was right there supporting us. We have a better time together when we're all happy and feeling good about ourselves anyway. Our gratification was delayed, not dismissed. Gratification doesn't always have to be instant, and in our case, waiting was worth it.

CHANGING FOR THE BETTER

There are women who are so disciplined and work so hard to live a healthy lifestyle; yet when they're around friends who struggle with weight loss, they may choose to slack off a bit to appease their friends and not make them uncomfortable. If these are your real friends, they will commend you for being able to do something that they find difficult. You will inspire them, not make them jealous. They will want to learn from you and you will motivate and assist them on their journey without mockery or patronization because you want to see your friends do well. We all have moments when we're up and moments when we're down. We all have wins and we all experience losses. Don't presume that your girlfriends are only there for the easy or fun stuff. Don't suppose that because you're all women, they can somehow read your mind. We have to communicate and trust that our friends won't be judgmental or combative. It's not always about what we say, but how we say it that makes a difference.

Maybe you have a friend you called all the time while you were single and didn't have any kids. You may have gotten laid off from work, but then things turned around in your life. You're working more. A new guy, or even a husband and some kids might be in the picture now. You don't call that friend as much anymore, not because you don't want to, but because sometimes you're exhausted after a long day. Then one day, that friend tells other people that you've changed ever since you've got these new things going on in your life. She tells everybody else how she feels, but she doesn't tell you. Then she acts weird and has an attitude every time you call her - almost hostile. She avoids you, or worse, she acts like everything is completely normal.

At certain stages in our lives, we will encounter those friends who don't seem to understand. Growth is essential to change, especially when that change is for the better - like when it turns an immature, irresponsible girl into a mature, decisive, and confident woman. There should be no negative connotation on the word "change." You only needed a ride before because you didn't have your own car. You only had all that extra time to spend on the phone with that friend because you had little going on. You haven't changed into a terrible friend because your circumstances got better. Now, you can choose to retaliate and start going back and forth about how much you've done for her. You can play tit for tat and compare who did more, calling her petty and jealous and throwing away your friend, or you can choose to communicate to her that those were not your intentions and that you appreciate and love her for always being there for you. Have a sincere conversation that humbles you both. Share your wins without bragging. Let her know what's happening in your life. Believe it or not, she doesn't hate or even dislike you. Your friend isn't mad because she believes you've changed for the worst. She's hurt because she doesn't feel like she is a part of that journey anymore. She misses her friend. When people care about you, they want to cheer for you. They want to be there for that ride with you. Sometimes, they are too proud to tell you they miss you and they need you.

When women are being hateful about your attempts to improve yourself and your life, ponder whether those women are your real friends and if they have your best interest at heart. I'm not naïve. I know that there are women who may never change their ways, women who are okay feeling the way they feel and having the relationships they do with other women. Go where you're wanted and where you can affect the most change. Don't force toxic relationships, and don't try converting haters into fans, especially at the cost of losing who you are. Sisters should be there through it all. Yes, sometimes feelings will get hurt, but we must listen and hear each other out. Take responsibility and apologize, even when it feels like the hardest thing to do; make a commitment not to do it again and create a plan to help avoid repeating the same mistakes. It can be a challenge to distinguish between these types of women sometimes, and it can be even more challenging to admit that sometimes we are that type of woman. The good news is, no matter where you fall, you have free will and can pivot.

We know what the problems are. We live with the symptoms every day. But where did this begin and how do we stop it? This is one of those times when I don't feel bad saying, "It's not all our fault." Or is it? Let's examine a potential root cause and address the source.

WHAT WE'RE TAUGHT

Many of us didn't learn how to handle defeat, rejection, or change. A lot of us had constant exposure to thoughtless arguments among surrounding women, yet seldom were we exposed to thoughtful resolution. Growing up in my small village, it took a community to raise a child. I could get my little behind whooped by an older woman unrelated to me. If my mother and another woman did not get along, I could not pass that woman on the streets without saying good morning, afternoon, or evening. If a grown woman asked me a question or warned me not to do something, I would be in big trouble with my mother if I gave that other woman any sort of attitude or backtalk. There was punishment for making fun of someone with a disability. I couldn't mock someone slow in learning, someone who lost a parent, or someone who had even less than I did. My mother was no joke. I couldn't go around disrespecting other people without repercussions.

She was also a woman of faith, and I used to wonder why she would repeat some of the same things when she prayed. As children, we absorb so much, whether or not we intend to. I started mimicking some things that I learned through repetition from my mom's prayers. Sometimes I would even mock her.

"Well mommy, maybe if you asked God for some new stuff instead of the same old things you keep praying for, we would have more things."

Silly little rabbit I was. Her response was always swift and shrewd. She'd tell me to hush up so fast that my lips would invert. Now that's being tight-lipped. My mom never ended a prayer without asking for humility, grace, and strength. I didn't know what those words meant back then. Here's the thing: she always knew where she fell short and she prayed for help where she knew she needed it the most. That woman is my inspiration and one of the best teachers I could ever ask for.

I was quite active in elementary school; I played netball, ran track, and wasn't afraid to run around. I would climb trees, fall and bruise myself, hop on tractors, and play in the dirt. I was a girl's girl, but I also loved the independence of climbing a tree for my own mangoes and guavas or burrowing into the sugarcane fields and breaking off the perfect piece for myself. I didn't wait around for the boys to do it for me; I wanted to trample the fields along-side them. Why should they have all the fun? I never picked up on any gender biases in class. I was in a classroom with boys five days a week. We girls learned the same things they were learning by the same teachers they were being taught by. Even at home, my mom gave me and my younger brother similar chores. I had to do most of it sometimes, but only because I was the eldest sibling in the house.

Outside of those two domains, a different lesson was being taught, one that seemed to be more cultural. Girls needed to learn how to cook, clean, take care of a home, children, a man, and herself, and look pretty doing it all. Women also needed to learn how to be independent of men. One might say that sends an indirect message that women shouldn't expect men to be able to provide for and protect them. Thus, we should prepare for the worst and hope for the best, as if men had proven to be inconsistent or incapable.

Nothing appeared to confirm this independence more than having material things. I saw grown women fighting each other in the streets over men — the same men they were being taught to expect lower standards from. Jealousies often intensified. This led to arguments, even more so when a man dared to defy those low expectations. When a woman could be a homemaker because the man in her life provided for her, this seemed to stir bitterness and anger from other women. As a young girl, you can only imagine the confusing message this all created. Grown women would quarrel and measure their successes against another based on whose house was the largest or best decorated. Women cursed each other over whose child was the brightest or whose new boyfriend was the shiniest. What in the world was going on? Heavy-handed insults were being traded back and forth. Hands waved about in each other's faces and sometimes dresses got tossed up. Someone would say something that was too insulting to bear and then — Slap! A full-on brawl would follow. The children were bystanders of these lionesses on hind legs battling in the jungle — hot, angry, and focused on ripping into each other.

This wasn't only happening within my culture, though. It was happening in many other places on many levels, in similar and different ways. In some places, girls could not play sports or engage in anything competitive. Some were not even offered the opportunity to enter classrooms or get an education. It's not only about cultures either.

Some girls were brought up in families teaching them not to be overachievers; meanwhile, others had to seek perfection and settle for nothing less, no matter what it took or who they had to step on. Some girls were taught that their beauty is everything, and it puts them above other women. Others were told that they were unattractive and shouldn't set their standards too high. Some women were taught to raise their voices and argue loudly, proudly, and without a filter. Others were taught that ladies should be soft spoken, that women who raise their voices are masculine and vulgar. Some women learned that it's rude to talk about what you have in front of those who have less, while others learned never to hide their accomplishments for anyone to feel better. Some women were taught not to trust or count on other women. In other places, women learned to work together as a community. In some circumstances, women were taught that there was a limit to what they could achieve, as others were taught that there was nothing they couldn't excel at. Don't depend on a man; you must be independent and never have to answer to a man. This was the lesson drilled into some women's minds. For others, it was learning how to be good homemakers, or working hard and getting an education while also being encouraged to find a good husband who would provide for and take care of his family, as is his manly duty .

All across the world, social, religious, and cultural influences teach girls how to exist, as well as how they should perceive those who differ from them. These misconceptions pass down through generational bloodlines, but not all women are the same — an obvious fact. Another fact is that we should accept and celebrate these differences, especially when they are responsible for the values that make us good people.

If a girl is competitive and she has a healthy outlet to express that side of herself, it may not only teach her the principles in winning with humility and for the right causes; it could teach her the valuable lessons in losing with dignity as well.

When they teach us such disparate and perplexing lessons, is the divide a genuine mystery to anyone? The way society looks at each other's differences with contempt, fear, and intolerance doesn't confuse me anymore. Many of us learned these attitudes and never questioned if there might be another way to look at things. Trying to understand each other still hasn't even occurred to some people. How do you treat a woman who wasn't raised to be as ambitious as you? How do you treat a woman who learnt to be unsympathetic to the misfortunes of others? How do you treat a woman who was taught to look down on those who don't look like her, or come from where she comes from? How do you treat a woman who has it ingrained that she needs to be loud in order to be heard?

Rarely do we try to find out why someone behaves the way they do. Instead, we presume and judge. It's much easier to categorize or dismiss people altogether. None of us choose the families or cultures that we are born into. We are no better than the other woman who does things the way she learned them. The only difference between us is opportunities. We can teach a universal lesson right now: our lives don't matter more than hers, and she deserves the same basic human rights as we do. We won't stand by and watch other women being abused and bullied, and we won't be the perpetrators of these acts, either. We must not look down on her because she believes, acts, feels, or looks differently. There's a lot we could all stand to win by learning from each other.

Take the time to get to know a person. Get to know her story before you judge her choices. We make excuses for ourselves and those we care for all the time. Let it be the same for other women, within reason. Exhaust every benefit of the doubt before thinking the worst of another woman. If someone says something nasty about her or starts a rumor, be quick to question it, debunk it, or simply ignore it . Don't fan the flame by repeating the story, sharing it on your social media platforms, or thinking badly about this person. If it's not important enough to you to find out the truth or the reason behind something, then it's not important enough to dwell on it or repeat it. Let's not waste any more time judging each other because we don't all think or act the same way.

We are all works in progress, and there is so much that we can learn from each other when we come together with open hearts and minds, and share the stories that led to our individualities and similarities.

I HAD THE PRIVILEGE TO VISIT SOUTH AFRICA AND VOLUNTEER AT A girls' orphanage a few years ago. I met a lady outside of my mission one day. Her name was Lilah, and she was old enough to be my grandmother — a very well preserved one at that. She was courteous and poised, with a meek but vibrant and charming personality. We struck up a conversation, as we were the only two women outside at the time. It began with small talk about where we were from and how I was liking Africa so far. I learned that she was from Cameroon and had recently moved to South Africa with her family. While we spoke, another lady by the name of Grace glided up toward us. She was unassertive and twelve years younger than Lilah. They were both stunning women with wide set eyes and thick, beautiful, dark brown hair. They had the most luminous skin that appeared to be dipped in a perfect concoction of cinnamon and gold. They had the most inviting smiles.

Based on the trading of hugs, I assumed they were sisters or, at the very least, very good friends. Lilah introduced us without hesitation, and Grace joined in on our conversation. Curiosity got the better of me and I asked if they were relatives.

With a slight tilt of the head and a gentle smile, Lilah answered, "Grace is from the old village I grew up in and she's my co-wife."

My reaction was crude at best. I tried covering up the confused look on my face with an even more confused grin. Lilah, being as sharp as she was, caught me. I could tell she wasn't shocked or offended by my reaction, though.

She commented in the most delicate and reassuring manner, "Child, don't worry. These things are misunderstood and frowned upon where you come from, so I understand."

I wanted to say, "Oh no girl, you most certainly don't."

I hadn't been that curious, nervous, and eager in a long time. I could barely keep calm as I rambled, "You must help me understand it."

She began explaining the misconceptions and judgments that often came her way. "Contrary to what some cultures might have you believe, a man having a second wife is not always about sexual conquests."

Lilah's story went like this:

Old traditions where she grew up many years ago gave men the right to have more than one wife. It's not a well-kept secret that many past kings had several wives. Most of the time this was due to high infant mortality rates, which threatened a king's desire to have heirs. Kings wanted to have many heirs to carry on their legacies. It was also because they lacked certain medical knowledge that we have today. For fear of causing miscarriages, many kings avoided sexual relations with their wives during the months of pregnancy. This left them naturally yearning for physical companionship. Although many kings in other countries and cultures took on mistresses, in Lilah's culture, they took another wife. This act made the king responsible for the other woman. She was not used and discarded as many mistresses in some other societies were. As a wife, this woman had rights, wealth, and land. She was looked after and provided for as his first wife was. Beyond the reasons of kings, the average man would also marry another woman to expand his family and means. Several wives were seen as a sign of social status and wealth. If a man had multiple wives, it meant that he had the wealth to support them. It also showed that he possessed the stamina to keep them all satisfied. I asked her how so many women could be provided for by the average man who was not a king. She explained that marrying more than four women was not permissible.

"They each have to be honored equally. What he provides for one, he must be able to provide for all. He cannot show favoritism. If he cannot treat them all equally, then he must let them go in kindness. He cannot abuse them or mistreat them in any way. He cannot deny them their basic rights or anything else within reason. Most importantly, if he struggles to meet these expectations, he should only seek to have one wife. One wife is plenty enough for some men," she chuckled.

There was something else to it, something that I had not heard ever spoken about.

Within their community, women who were without husbands were often mistreated. Men were the maintainers and providers of their families. The women were encouraged to marry good husbands. That being said, Lilah made it abundantly clear that men and women not only understood their roles back then; they celebrated and took pride in them. Women were not trying to compete for mens' roles. They accepted their gender differences and celebrated them. Each gender appreciated the fact that they could do things the other couldn't. Men took pride in protecting and taking care of their family's financial needs. Women took pride in being homemakers, mothers, and the heart and soul of their communities. She said that men were as the veins within a body while the women were as the blood which pumped through those veins — no role was greater than the other, but no role was honored more than the wife and homemaker. Each one added value to the family. I was utterly intrigued.

Just then, Grace interrupted and decided that the next part of the story would be best told by her.

Grace had this look of humility and, dare I say, grace about herself in that moment. She told me that without a husband, some women resorted to prostitution. Many were ill-treated mistresses and others were abused and forgotten. Grace was one of those women.

She had two children by a man she was forced to marry at eighteen in order to clear a family debt. He later died and she had no home or wealth of her own. She struggled to take care of herself and her two children. She was sexually abused by a relative who had taken them in and had to leave. Grace wanted to be married to a gentle and loving man, but no one wanted to marry a woman with a reputation. To them, she was damaged, and two young children were a burden. She wasn't even a good candidate for the men who were known to have multiple wives. Grace was a God-fearing woman, as was Lilah. I could feel her faith and her heart in every unpretentious breath she took telling her story.

She began tearing up as she recounted the harshness people demonstrated toward her. We could see the pain overcoming Grace's demeanor. At that moment we all paused for a much-needed embrace. Then Lilah carried on by telling me that she actually met Grace while praying one day. Grace had her two kids tucked tightly beside her as she prayed. When she was done, Lilah walked over and struck up a conversation. The two women began talking and would regularly meet up with each other to pray from that point forward. During those meetings, Lilah would bring food, a little money, and blankets for Grace and her kids. The two ladies took an instant and genuine liking to each other, something I like to call a merging of two spectacular energies, or what some might call a connection.

"I saw myself in Grace," Lilah said. "I've been married for over three decades and have a wonderful husband who loves and provides for me. We had no children, although we had tried for many years to conceive." She cried softly, "I could never bear children."

It was the only time I noticed the tiny wrinkles perfectly set above her cheeks. They did nothing to detract from the beauty and elegance of her face. I was so humbled.

One day Lilah went to her husband with a request that still to this very day astounds me. She asked her husband to consider marrying Grace and providing a father for her two children. I knew that what I was hearing would be met with a hypercritical response if I ever repeated it to the women back home. The condemnation I felt these women would face in my society caused me to take a step back. I needed to reflect on my own misapprehensions.

Lilah had spoken of Grace to her husband once she learnt of Grace's circumstances. She convinced him that Grace and her two children would be no burden to them, that they had the space, the means, and the compassion to offer. She explained to him that Grace would also be able to contribute by helping her around the home. She then reminded him of the religious prophets who had multiple wives. Lilah didn't care about what anyone in her family or the community would say. Her husband took some time to think about what his wife had proposed. He was hesitant, but in time he agreed, although not before insisting that Grace and her kids come by for dinner. He was adamant that Grace should decide for herself if their home and family would make her and her children happy.

Grace was soon introduced to Lilah's husband. After witnessing his kindness and sharing her story with him, she chose to marry him. She was overjoyed. She and her children couldn't have been happier.

In Grace's own words, "It's easy for other cultures to judge. Once you have convinced yourself that you know best what someone else's intentions are, even the truth won't move you."

She said she was blessed to have not only a husband who had grown to love her and her children, but also to have a true friend and sister to walk the rest of life's journey with.

When I asked Lilah what made her do what she did, she said, ever so graciously, "It's simple, I want for my sister what I want for myself. What we choose to do with the blessings and the circumstances we're given is completely up to us."

As I gazed at their oval shaped faces, I couldn't stop myself from sobbing. I saw pain and experience. I saw survivors. I saw two women of great strength and courage. They had love and genuine respect for each other and it brought me to tears.

I still had a thousand burning questions for them both, but only one seemed important at the time. I asked, "So how long have you been a family?"

In the back of my mind I was clinically thinking, "There's no way this could last because women don't like to share a damn thing, much less their men."

"Nineteen years now."

I could have fainted when Grace replied. Now I needed to know how they navigated through all the typical ups and downs of marriage — having three different voices, opinions, attitudes, and personalities under one roof. I honestly couldn't imagine my spouse having to deal with two of me. God help him!

They both laughed as I joked about the headaches of having one woman, let alone two. They admitted that they had disagreements and different views on certain things, but what they had in common held the most weight — they both had faith. They both loved their family and were committed to keeping it together, and they both saw the value in each other. Lilah could have focused on the fact that Grace was younger and beautiful. She could have focused on the fact that Grace had two children when she couldn't have any. She could have scorned her or brought her into her home only to abuse her even further. Lilah saw beyond it all. She saw another woman who, under different circumstances, could have been her.

NOW YOU AND I CAN TRY TO TAKE THAT STORY, GO BACK TO THE beginning, and assume that we would have handled it differently and suggest the varying ways that Lilah should have chosen to help Grace. I did the same at first, when I asked if Lilah and her husband couldn't have taken Grace and her kids into their home without being co-wives. Grace was a woman who very much wanted to have a husband. She wanted companionship for herself as well as a father for her children. There are things we perceive to be sensible and normal behavior within our own cultures. Those same practices would make other cultures cringe. Who are we to judge what someone else feels and how they should exhibit an act of kindness? What if it was you; in that time, in that place, in those circumstances? It's easy to reject something we don't understand. Truth be told, I don't know if I'm a selfless enough woman to do that. I'd like to hope that I can be. I can appreciate and admire the fact that there are women who are. I respect them. None of us can judge whose society is being taught best when it comes to women and how we treat each other, or which society is correct. What I do know is that the messages are too often translated in ways that create division among women instead of opportunities for collaboration.

SEVEN
WE ARE THE TEACHERS

THERE IS AN OLD AFRICAN PROVERB WHICH STATES, "WHEN elephants fight, only the grass suffers." When we look at the attitudes that women and girls have toward each other, doesn't it frighten you? Doesn't it terrify you that a teenage girl out there, your daughter or your niece, is questioning if she's good enough? She's looking at herself and looking at the women on TV, the ones in music, in the magazines, on social media, and in her classroom. She is convinced that if she doesn't look like them, act like them, or have what they have, that she is somehow a loser: a failure, insufficient, too fat, too skinny, too pale, too dark, too poor, deficient, or ugly. Is it really all her fault? No, it unequivocally is not!

Little girls internalize the messages portrayed about women from TV, magazines, beauty pageants, their communities, and their homes, whether they realize it or not. It's not the intellect or the character that is being judged, it's their physical appearance. They are sexualized, celebrated, and then scrutinized. It upsets me at my very core. Instead of enjoying their childhoods, girls are picking themselves and their peers apart. Some of us will then label these girls, calling them weak, stupid, and insecure because they aren't able to cope with everything they're feeling. These are children navigating on a rudimentary level in a very adult world.

If that young girl hurts herself, her friend's mom might screech, "You need to stay away from that crazy, troubled girl."

If she decides that she's more comfortable being in a crowd of boys instead of girls, another mom might tell her daughter to stay away from that promiscuous or loose girl. I'm not asking a loaded question with a ridiculous premise to get affirmation that I'm right. Is it all their fault?

We tell girls one thing and then we show them another. We tell them that they are worth it and that they should be grateful for what they have. Meanwhile they are inundated with images and influences brainwashing them about needing more, convincing them that what they have isn't enough. The worst part is that it's women who are being used to portray and sell this life of excess to other women. This is what you should have to be on our level. This is what you should look like to attract men. This is how much money you should have to be successful and happy. This is the kind of car you should drive to appear important. These are the clothes you should wear and the house you should live in to be noticed and seen as somebody. When these things are not achieved, we can end with women who are not only displeased with themselves and severely depressed; they become resentful of other women for having those things.

CHANGE THE MESSAGE

The messages are so deceiving and convoluted. We don't realize we're being manipulated into supporting things meant to divide us even further. Women are actually vying for titles that degrade us, working overtime to be labeled as "bad bitches" and "boss bitches." How can we achieve sisterhood based on mutual love, respect, and understanding if we can't figure out how to love and respect ourselves first? Demanding that other women bow down to us and then calling them bitches doesn't encourage mutual respect. This dynamic breeds jealousy and hatred. Supporting each other is one thing; damn near worshiping and idolizing another person and placing them above yourself is quite another.

We are all beautiful, powerful forces of nature and we can choose not to use that against each other. While there is no shame or guilt in being successful, we can choose not to place ourselves above anyone else. We can choose to inspire another woman to be her best and most genuine self in spite of her circumstances, instead of killing her spirit because of them. We are all one bad mistake away from being locked up, one accident away from being crippled, one circumstance beyond our control from losing everything. None of us are infallible. We are our greatest asset.

Most of us judge not only strangers, but also those closest to us, including our own friends. We create these biases toward them based on the notion that women are catty and dramatic, that they won't understand, and they cannot keep a secret if their lives depended on it. We assume what they can and cannot handle and what they will or will not do for us. Many of us were told from a young age not to trust other girls, almost as much as we were told not to trust men. This is an extreme exaggeration and a detrimental view to impart on girls.

BE THAT WHICH YOU WISH TO SEE IN OTHERS

I saw the things that women bickered about and would even end friendships over. When men would cheat, women would turn on each other, even if the other woman did not know what that man was up to. We can't be so willing to hear out one guilty party and deny the other a fair opportunity to explain her side, calling her deplorable names and harboring hatred towards her (sometimes for years) while forgiving the man. We need to protect each other, even if we don't all know each other. Let's have each other's backs. One of the main reasons we may not trust other women has to do with the betrayals we have experienced. Be the type of woman that you hope another woman would be in the same situation.

This plague hasn't taken over all women. My mind and heart have shifted for the better. I credit the women who taught me through demonstration exactly what this sisterhood looks like, and what it has the potential to do in our individual lives. They taught me how it can change a society and even the world. As women, we are the designers of the lives we live — the architects of our society. We renovate, accessorize, and redecorate it to look and feel the way we want it to. We choose who we want to welcome in and who we don't. We take houses and turn them into homes; we take groceries and turn them into delicious full course meals. We take babies and nurture them into adulthood while holding to the possibility of progress and a better world for this generation of young women to inherit. It's in our hearts, heads, and hands.

I couldn't just talk about this anymore. This requires action. Talking about being trustworthy, compassionate, and understanding wasn't gonna cut it. We all needed to see what that looked like. More importantly, we needed to see the results of that work, because results matter. There is no perfect path to doing this, no perfect example, no quintessential woman who harbors no jealousy and passes no judgment. We only need to begin being better people to each other. I needed to start making the effort to change and be that better example - not a perfect one, but a better one, because I knew that I was capable of doing better, of being better. We all are, and I'm confident that we will.

Remember, we were not all being taught the same things. Some women may not be able to show you much compassion because none was ever shown toward them. They may have never seen what that looks like. It is impossible to teach someone else what one does not know. It is even harder to teach what one doesn't even realize they don't know, but there is more that connects us on a much deeper level than what separates us. Experiencing hurt or loss, feeling misunderstood, being judged or mistreated - there isn't a single woman who doesn't know what one or all of these feels like. There is so much more that connects us. Imagine living in a world where you were the only woman experiencing menstruation and trying to explain to people what you are going through. I'd be losing my damn mind because no one would understand. No one else would be able to relate to how I'm feeling. Eventually, they would probably succeed at making me think that I was crazy. The horror!

BE MINDFUL OF WHAT INFLUENCES YOU

The rivalry among us has gotten so thick that the rest of the world will tune in weekly to witness the outrageousness. The more salacious the content, the more views it gets and the more money it makes for those responsible. There is a world out there that is so unreal. It's so disconnected from reality, and yet it's the world that so many of us are choosing to connect with. Both young and old have become addicted to the internet and social media, so much so that we have become out of touch with how to connect in the real world — lacking empathy, forgiveness, and understanding because of this disconnect.

That world is designed with the intent to suck you in and maintain a hypnotic hold on you. We won't go five minutes without checking something, commenting on something, or posting something. Don't get me wrong; the internet and social media can be great tools when used for good. But how often has browsing social media only left you feeling empty, self-critical, and alone? It is one of the most divisive inventions ever created; and causes extreme life-altering pain for so many people, even while making the companies behind them billions. There is so much deception, but they keep you hooked by pretending as though your input is of significant importance when they don't care about what you have to say — especially when what you have to say opposes those things that positively affect their bottom line.

We are stubborn creatures of habit. We don't often admit that we are influenced by the imagery and content we choose to expose our minds to. It took a while to convince a friend that watching certain tv shows had influenced her in any way, even though her attitude and decision making showed signs of that over time. They were even shaping her opinions and changing the way she communicated, and not in a good way. It took some real self-reflecting and catching a glimpse of herself on a recorded video for her to admit that she was seeing more of those women in her own behavior. She didn't like it one bit. She went from being able to have civil disagreements to never wanting an argument or debate to end, or at least until she felt like she had won, all while talking with her hands waving in front of your face (something she never did before). Now, seeing other women's weaknesses exploited for gain, watching them argue, curse, and tear down one another for fame or wealth while checking off the list of every stereotype already placed on women, wasn't so amusing to her anymore. She no longer wanted to support that form of female exploitation or degradation.

Introducing a new concept, especially to grown women, isn't always the easiest thing; however, it's possible with consistency. When I stopped expecting people to change and I began to work on my own deficiencies, that's when it happened — those small improvements and mind shifts began laying a foundation for new habits. We learn through repetition. I was determined to repeat better habits. I'm still trying, still learning, and still a work in progress. Every day, when I think of the world of women out there who need it, I do my best to show support, love, compassion, tolerance, trust, and understanding, even at the risk of sounding like a broken record to the ones closest to me.

Old habits need to be replaced. Don't mock other women's insecurities. Don't judge them before you know their story. Don't criticize because her way is different from yours. We don't know the "why" behind the choices each individual makes. Make time for your friends when they need you most. Uplift them and check in on them just to make sure they're feeling and doing well. Remind them of how capable and incredible they are and create a safe space of trust.

MAKE A HABIT OF CHANGING FOR THE BETTER

I decided that I needed to work on being the change I wanted to see in others. That's when I began seeing the change within myself, but also in the women in my life. This requires us to accept that we can do better and begin implementing little things each day. The women in my life may not even have realized how much they actually helped me during my own process. This is not something we master in a week, a month, or even a year. It's a lifelong commitment to being the person that we want others to be to us. We're not perfect; we will sometimes fall short of doing the right thing. We'll still get hurt, disappointed, angry, sad, and furious. The difference is that now we can begin to arm ourselves with the tools to overcome some of our worst impulses — tools like patience, understanding, forgiveness, and love.

Remember that who someone reveals themself to be shouldn't change who you are. You know you are better than retaliation. You know that you are trustworthy. You know that you may regret your words and actions. You know that doing that isn't the best option to resolve the matter. Starting a rumor about another woman because she hurt us shouldn't cross our minds. Wishing ill on her only delays or blocks good from coming to us much sooner. If you love someone, you always leave room in hope that they may find their way back to a friendship with you. Don't burn the bridge that could lead back to friendship.

It all comes down to how we choose to look at other women. We cannot control the actions of another; we can only influence and inspire them. How we choose to react to things is completely within the scope of our control. It's not all our fault, but there is something we can do about it. First of all, we can end the cycle of misguided and harmful teachings upon young girls. We must not perpetuate these divisive messages. Secondly, we need to unlearn some of what we were taught. We do that by overriding the impulses of old habits forcing their way to the surface with new and better ones. Lastly, we've got to be kinder, more tolerant and patient with ourselves and each other, one day at a time, one change at a time, and woman at a time.

EIGHT
YOU ARE YOUR ONLY
COMPETITION

I USUALLY LOVE AN IDEA OR I HATE IT, BUT I'VE ALWAYS TUSSLED with ambivalence over the rivalry amongst women. Is this female rivalry even a real thing? Some of you may very well deny its existence altogether and think women get along perfectly well with each other. Then why do so many women still insist that they don't or barely have female friends, or that they prefer having men as friends because they are less dramatic and don't talk as much?

The actual battle we face is with ourselves. So many women have experienced the constraints of internal conflict. It's sometimes difficult for us to exhibit our competitive sides. We risk being ridiculed or ostracized if we show too much of our strength, or even our sexuality. Some women may limit themselves so they don't ruffle any feathers or make others uncomfortable. Some also remain quiet to avoid the common, "she's too this," or, "she thinks she's so that," comments. Subsequently, that can lead to insecurities and jealousy over other women's abilities to go against that grain or to live outside of society's standards of what's normal and acceptable. Women are usually the caretakers of the family, putting everyone else's needs before their own. Most women are lovers and nurturers by nature. We actually care about other people, including other women. The competition is not what women really want, nor does it make anyone happy. It's how some women cope with the underlying competition they are having with themselves, the projection of insecurities, fears, and self-doubt onto other women. It can reveal women's frightened instinct to protect themselves. They want protection from aiming at success and failing, protection from being seen as too much of an aggressor, too successful, or too powerful by other women in case they offend, hurt, or upset them. Believe it or not, women don't actually enjoy being hated by other women.

Ambitious, intelligent, and hardworking are not traits we should minimize. Women don't need to silence themselves regarding their abilities and accomplishments. Making yourself invisible so that others can feel seen will only lead to depression and unhappiness. We should encourage healthy competition. Doing your best and wanting to outdo your personal best isn't a bad thing. Women become unsatisfied with what they have, what they can do, and who they are when they compare their efforts to that of other women. We are no longer competing against each other, but we are battling with ourselves. We're losing our confidence because our best doesn't look like someone else's. Women want to be perceived as these multifaceted jugglers in life's circus, handling everything and everyone and never dropping the ball. News flash! Everyone drops a ball or two now and again. We can be so hard on ourselves that it becomes impossible for us to be supportive of other women's successes, because we don't know how to be happy with our own. Success can take on many forms. Decide what that looks like to you. If it's money, fame, and power, then you have it in you to work your butt off and achieve that. Whether it's raising a family and sending incredible adults out into society or feeding the poor and living your life in service of others, do it. You determine what success looks like in your life and then go for it!

It's so easy to become fixated on trying to achieve a life similar to someone else's, so much so that we become strangers in our own lives. The other issue is trust. When you hurt another woman, understand that you have made it harder for her to trust other women. Her distrust of other women will then cause them not to trust her either. No one likes the person who only absorbs but shares nothing in return. Teach people how to trust you by being trustworthy, by showing forgiveness and compassion, by being rational, fair-minded, and objective. We sometimes associate the character traits of one woman to all other women we find similar to her. The envy often peaks so high that women will convince others to judge another woman to feel validated, drawing lines in the sand before even getting to know the person. Betrayal is never a simple thing, but we can overcome it. Allow others the opportunity to gain your trust and do it with a clear and genuine heart. Allow others to see the value of trusting you and you trusting them. As human beings, we look but don't always see. We must start truly seeing each other as human beings - people who hurt, feel, cry, get sad, and go through hardships and loneliness like we ourselves do. Recognize that you might feel misunderstood because you have misunderstood someone else.

Two years into a marriage, I sat apprehensively awaiting my doctor's return to the medical room. It was only a couple of weeks earlier that they gave me an ultrasound and a few other tests. They placed a dye into the area to show the doctor where the problem was and how big of a problem it was. With her face set, my doctor patrolled into the room. She explained that my left fallopian tube was blocked beyond repair. It had to be removed.

Surgery? I was only thirty years old. I was trying to conceive a child. The feeling of trepidation was immediate. I went from emotional to angry and then frightened. What if it's worse than we imagine and I lose my entire uterus? What if my husband resents me? What if I can never have a child? What if something goes wrong and I don't wake up? What will my friends and family think?

I stigmatized myself. Each time I would see a mother doing something I wouldn't do as a mom or hear a story about child abuse, I became angry. I compared myself to those women and wondered why I wasn't so blessed. I was so depressed looking up cases online, even after countless reassurances from my doctor that it was not a worst-case scenario. She said I still had a fifty-fifty chance of getting pregnant the old-fashioned way with one fallopian tube. None of that mattered to me. Her words kept rolling off my ears like raindrops on a petal. They were about to remove a part of what made me a woman and that's all that registered in my mind.

Over the waiting period before surgery day, I began feeling less feminine. I felt very unappealing and my self-worth was diminishing. I told no one — not even my family. I doubted they would understand. Up to that point, I had only contacted my fertility specialist. The next appointment was to discuss selecting a surgery date and the surgeon. They were about to learn of my immense, borderline psychotic fear of being under anesthesia, made worse by the fact that my neighbor had only recently undergone a procedure where she had to go under anesthesia; upon waking up, her male surgeon commented that her body was beautiful. She wasn't in there for a cosmetic procedure, so she found the comment quite unprofessional and disturbing. She was married and didn't appreciate it at all. You can imagine how that story only solidified my fears and added another layer to my hysteria. I emphatically requested to have a female surgeon. I went even further by requesting an all-female team. If I was going to be naked and knocked the heck out, I would rather have a bunch of women over me than some strange men.

My doctor put in the request, laughing the entire time at my dramatics. She told me not to get my hopes up about the all-female team. The anesthesiologist on duty that day could be male, and that was a decision made by the hospital. She confirmed my surgeon would be female. Well, I could live with that.

Fast forward to two months later. Surgery day, I showed up exhausted. I had slept little the night before; I was too anxious. I staggered into the hospital, checked in, and prepared for what was to come. There wasn't a single soul who encountered me that morning who couldn't smell the fear on me. I was petrified and my emotions were doing sprints that could have qualified me for the Olympics. Once I got to the patient waiting area where they separate you from other patients by a curtain, one by one each of the nurses made their way in and introduced themselves, said some calming words, and exited. Shortly after, they all returned together, along with my surgeon and the anesthesiologists. Oh yeah, all women! I was elated.

The team gave me a rundown of what was about to happen and did their best to reassure me that everything was going to be okay. Word had spread that I was a nervous wreck. They all left, and Dr. Butin, the surgeon, stuck her head back through the curtain.

With the most generous and calming smile, she said, "You're gonna soldier through this, I can tell, and I'm going to be here every step of the way. I've got you."

I hadn't believed a single word of reassurance about that surgery since day one, but for whatever reason, I believed her. About 35 minutes later, they were ready for me. I was being rolled down a lit hallway on a white linen covered bed. It smelled like an odd mixture of linen scented Febreze and Bengay. This is where my life, my perspective, and my entire attitude about women shifted.

As one nurse carefully pushed the bed forward, another moseyed alongside me saying, "Don't be nervous, you're in the best hands."

Another inched closer to the bed and said, "Keep calm, she knows what she's doing."

Suddenly, not only did I believe these women I had just met without them having to prove anything to me; I believed in them as well.

The nurse pushing the bed added, "It's okay to be nervous, but we're all right here with you."

That was the moment I turned my head around, tilted it back and saw the most spectacular demonstration of power and purpose that I had ever seen. It was a team of women. They were confident, compassionate, strong, brilliant, capable, and they were all there to help me — to support me and make sure I would make it through that day.

THESE INCREDIBLE WOMEN WERE ON MY TEAM. ONCE WE GOT INTO the room, Dr. Butin greeted me again. She introduced the team once more and clarified what everyone's job was going to be. They were like a well-oiled machine or a perfectly synced sports team — each one with a task, none more important than the other, yet all codependent on each other and not competing for each other's roles. There was no ego present. You would have thought that I was already under anesthesia. I felt such tranquility. I knew in that moment that whatever happened, by God's work and through their hands, I was safe. Once on the surgical table, they hooked me up, masked me up, and then we joked for a bit. They asked me to count backwards from ten; I recall getting to eight. It was all chocolate cupcake dreams from there.

Many things changed for me on that table. During the surgery, Dr. Butin found scar tissue around the remaining fallopian tube. There was too much to save or repair. There was nothing she could do but remove it. Had she left it inside me, I would have been back on that table in less than six months, losing my entire uterus or worse. I went into surgery to remove one fallopian tube. The decision to remove them both fell to the discernment of another woman, a doctor — a stranger who was asked by my husband, "What would you want your husband to do if it was you in there?"

I woke up a few hours after surgery to the same team of women by my side. My first words were, "chocolate cupcakes." They all started laughing, but then their happy expressions changed almost instantly. One of them was rubbing my head and wiped my face because I was sweating so much. The others held my hands as Dr. Butin described the events that took place in the operating room. The devastating news sent a flood of tears rushing down my face.

Both my tubes were gone. How? Why? I was healthy. I took care of myself; I followed all the rules and didn't do anything that wasn't conducive to being healthy. My option for having kids was now reduced to one: in-vitro fertilization, also known as IVF. As I write this, my hands tremble while remembering the inconsolable pain I felt. In my mind, my body had failed me; or I had failed it; somehow. I couldn't understand how this could happen to me.

Dr. Butin excused herself and soon after, the other women one by one followed. Before being discharged, Dr. Butin popped back in one last time. She affirmed that she meant what she said and she would be there every step of the way. She provided me with her contact information and hugged me. I thanked her again for the amazing and difficult job she did.

The first week was the worst. I was writhing in physical pain, made all the worse by my emotional pain. The emotional pain was the most excruciating. Dr. Butin called to check on me during that first week and we spoke on the phone at least once a day. She continued checking on me because of the deep state of depression I had fallen into. My confidence was non-existent. It embarrassed me to tell my friends and family, so I isolated myself. I was in no rush to deal with the awkward question that had already been thrown at me for years.

"So, when are you planning on having kids?"

I had already dealt with the uncomfortable subject a few years prior when a relative accused me of not getting pregnant because she thought I was one of "those women," who doesn't want to ruin her figure. They also criticized me when I didn't immediately get pregnant after marrying.

I felt like disappearing into myself. I felt like half of a woman, and there was nothing anyone could do or say to make me feel any different. I became angry. What made it worse was that my husband began to resent me as well. I felt inadequate. In his eyes, I didn't do the most basic thing that a woman should do: procreate. I was terrified of jumping into IVF (in-vitro), because I felt like my body had let me down once and that it would do so again. I ate healthy, exercised, prayed daily, and wasn't a drinker or smoker. I didn't live a fast-paced or outgoing lifestyle. I convinced myself that maybe I didn't deserve a family.

I was too young to help keep my parents together when they went their separate ways. Now I could not start my own family. I was afraid of trying and failing. My body had become unpredictable. I couldn't trust it. I wasn't mentally strong enough to handle another disappointment so soon. My self-esteem bore a hole through the ground and sealed itself off with cement. I didn't see my family or friends for the next 2 years.

A few weeks later, I went in for my follow up appointment. Dr. Butin presented me with a beautiful bouquet, including a hand-written note. She was ecstatic to see me on my feet with so much strength and energy. She was also excited about the bamboo arrangement I got her as a thank you. I guess we were both of the same mind that day; however, the appointment took a turn. It became somewhat of a therapy session.

We had been talking more often for weeks. I soon realized that we had, in fact, been laying the foundation for what would become a friendship. I confided to her that a friend had recently given birth and I was so filled with jealousy. My friend invited me to a baby welcoming party. I felt it best to stay away and not have my negative energy cloud her moment of joy.

Dr. Butin and I talked for over two hours and even cried together. She marched up to the emotional door I had sealed off from everyone and kicked it down until it crumbled. She kept reminding me of the team of women who stood by me during my surgery. They had my back when I was scared. She explained that each person's role is going to be different, like each person's path in life will be different. She emphasized that whenever I was ready, whether or not I decided to do IVF, that the role I chose wouldn't be any less. I wouldn't be any less than anyone fulfilling a different role.

It was such a profound scene. I sat there soaking in all the wisdom she offered in her delicate delivery. I understood that even though my friend was a new happy mom, motherhood comes with its own set of fears. I needed to have my friend's back now, like the team of women at the hospital that day had mine. I was brave, strong, imperfect, and I was not alone.

She concluded, "You can allow yourself to be there for your friend because I'm going to be here for you."

In two hours, all the anger and blame I was carrying for myself, and even toward her, was all but gone. It took a few more of those conversations to bring me back, but I am so grateful. She shared a gift of love and understanding with me. There were no egos involved. Here was a woman who gave me her word that she had my back in this, and she kept it. She was never too busy to take or return a phone call. She was a doctor who became my therapist, friend, and sister.

The day before she left for vacation, she swung by and we drove to the hospital together. I wanted to give the team of women who'd also had my back that day some homemade chocolate cupcakes. You didn't think we forgot about my chocolate cupcake dreams, did you?

The respect, the love, and the kindness they showed me will remain engraved in my memory and in my heart. How could a surgeon with hundreds of patients care about me enough to invest in my life in the way she did? I wasn't so special. Yet she referred to me as being like a sister because of how we had grown to communicate with one another. I trusted her, respected her, and appreciated her as she had come to admire my strength and the courage it took to overcome my depression. At a time when I needed to feel safe, a time where I could have deflected my insecurities, blame, and fears onto her, she showed me through her words and actions that I was safe with her. This was the friendship that repaired my inner strength.

IT'S NOT AN ANOMALY

What I realized was that these shifts were happening all over the world. Women appreciate other women. Women are trusting other women and supporting other women. It only takes one act of kindness. Be that woman that makes other women feel safe in your presence. No one else will ever come close to being a worthy enough opponent in the competition. The worthiest opponent is you. It will never change or get better until you realize that. Keep doing your best. Keep trying to be better than you were yesterday, if that's what makes you happy. The goal is to be happy no matter what your best looks like. Your competition is you. You can access all the tools within yourself to always come in first place.

I HAD BEEN VISITING SOME RELATIVES ON THE ISLAND OF ST. Maarten. After days of sarcasm, condescending commentary, and feeling extremely unwelcome, we reached an impasse in communication. I was confiding in a friend abroad who informed his cousin Shara about what was going on. Shara lived on the island, but we had never met. Yet upon his request, she called me. I told her where I was and in a matter of twenty minutes, she was outside.

He asked her to check on me to make sure I was okay. She had the most magnanimous energy and confidence haloed over her. My initial assumptions were dubious at best. I was mortified and couldn't stop myself from thinking, "This woman must think I'm pathetic."

I thought of how inconvenient she must have felt at that moment. She exuded such confidence and showed quite a genuine concern for me. It took less than ten minutes for her to assess the situation and determine that she was going to pull off a one-woman rescue mission.

We got my things and she peeled out of there. You would think that I was related to her or had known her for years. She didn't care whose fault it was or wasn't. She saw the disappointment, humiliation, and exhaustion on my face. That was enough for her to decide that she was only going to focus on how to change that. Driving to the hotel with purpose but not hurriedly, she asked what had happened. I explained in more detail what was going on. She told me that her cousin called her to check on me and get me out of there if necessary. I had almost two weeks left before I was scheduled to return home. It was frustrating. I would have already been back home two weeks prior, but I extended my stay after my relatives begged me to stay longer since it had been a while since my last visit. So you can imagine how upsetting it was, having to change my flight once again.

I couldn't believe that this woman left her job early and came to a complete stranger's rescue. There was something about her that felt safe, trusting. Her compassion fused with her demeanor of assertiveness instantly made me feel better. Once we got to the hotel, she made sure I was safe, secure, and settled. We decided to get dinner and we talked some more.

I realized two things about her. The first was that she was extremely loyal to those who were loyal to her. It explained why she went out of her way for me when her cousin asked her to. They were very close. Secondly, she was unapologetically transparent in the best way. What you saw was what you got. No frills, no games, no pretenses. The next morning, she called to check on me and decided to stop by after work. We went out to eat and ended up sharing almost our entire life stories with each other.

That same night she invited me out with some friends of hers and I accepted. Saying that we had a blast would be an understatement. I forgot all about how my trip had gone before meeting her. I was about to change my flight the next day so I could finally return home. Shara stressed that there was no need for that. I didn't need to let what happened with my relatives chase me off the island and ruin my vacation. She insisted that I stay at her place until the end of my trip.

I don't know what would have happened had I changed my flight. What I do know is that everything happens for a reason. Everyone we meet, good or bad, shows up in our lives with a purpose to either test us, help us, break us, or restore us. This was the friendship that restored my trust and hope in women. There are phenomenal females out there who see no point to the competition. They want all women to be treated well, to be dealt with fairly, and to be able to use our voices to help one another instead of tearing each other down.

APPRECIATE THE GREATNESS IN EACH OTHER

I had the most incredible time with a stranger who I now call sister. She opened up her home and heart to me and introduced me to her friends and family, who also embraced me. I could definitely see and feel where her acceptance and generosity came from. I was twenty-six and she was thirty. She made it so easy for me to share my dreams, aspirations, and motivations. She encouraged and commended me on the things that I was doing and still wanted to do in my life.

It would have been so easy for me to be jealous of her independence, her attitude, and her accomplishments, but my self-transformation had already begun. She cared about me, looked out for me like a little sister. She listened to me, advised me, she made me feel safe and not judged. She inspires me to this day still. How could I envy someone I had grown to respect and love? Simply put, I couldn't. It took some time, self-reflecting, and growth to get to a point where acknowledging the greatness in other women actually made me proud to be one. I see their greatness as a reflection not of who I am per se, but of what I am capable of, of what we are all capable of. Our greatness is undeniable, and no one woman has monopoly over it. The goal shouldn't be to seek strati-fication. We don't have to be famous to be counted, protected, appreciated, respected, and loved. These basic needs which we all share make us equal, with more in common than what separates us.

NINE
GO EASY ON YOURSELF AND EACH OTHER

HOW LONG CAN YOU PRETEND TO BE SOMEONE YOU'RE NOT? ONCE you're busted and people see through the facade, you only have two options: either hold on to that persona and defend it to the bitter end, or lay down the pretenses and show the world the real you.

People who are not authentic will often find it more difficult to build genuine connections. Allow yourself to be seen, truly. It's frustrating for everyone involved when we hide the truth about ourselves. However, considering the pain that every woman has experienced for being exactly who we are, it's no wonder so many of us create alter egos according to who we're around. It's our defense mechanism. Our brain doesn't want us to get hurt or feel pain. The moment we're in an environment with any perceived threat, the brain responds to protect us, usually by signaling whether or not to proceed with caution by producing fear — fear of letting that person in, fear of getting too close. When we see other women as our sisters instead of competition, we're retraining the brain, giving it new data to store. By improving that data, we change the initial response to each other. What was once a presumed threat or caution is now a non-threat or friend. We have to change our minds about each other.

We may fight with our sisters, but through it all, we love them past the pain and any disappointment. We have a natural inclination to protect them, support them, and help them in any way we can. None of these matter, though, unless you figure out who you are first. Pretending to be someone you're not is a waste of time. Human beings are notorious for being fickle. With our ever-changing minds, what do you care if they don't like something about you today? You don't always like everything about yourself. If it becomes popular tomorrow and you're still doing it, guess what — now they love it. It's so exhausting. By the time you figure out which identity to take up next, they have already changed their minds on what's cool or acceptable and what isn't.

Remain consistent with being you. Stay true to who you are. At some point, the needle on the spinning social wheel of acceptance will land on what you're doing. They'll catch up. You never throw out that pair of jeans that no one wears anymore. You keep it because you know that at some point it's going to be in style again. People are changing their minds about what's acceptable right now. Morals and principals get weighted. Still, they sometimes seem to lose in the popularity contest.

Tap into your power by seeing yourself, your true self, and claim your moment to self-transform. Pivot and choose a different course than the one you've grown accustomed to. There is beauty in the pain you have experienced. Use it to fuel you in a positive direction. Figure out what you want for your own life. Write it down and reject any idea that challenges that amazing perception you have of yourself. Write it down and free it from inside your mind and soul. Get to know yourself. Don't be a stranger to yourself. Think about what makes you unique. Figure out what you're passionate about and what you can give to yourself, your family, and this world in a way that only you can. If you can't figure out your passion, start here. What would you continue doing with your life tomorrow if you woke up with ten million dollars in the bank? What is that thing that would remain consistent in your life because you love doing it and you're good at it? That's your passion.

Let your passion feed your purpose. Your purpose is how you use your passion in service to yourself and others. How can you improve not only your life, but also affect another person's life positively? That's the purpose. It will take work — inner work. So, get to work. Work for it, and keep working every day. It's easy to become complacent. Working on who you are and being happy with that woman in the mirror is the key to this and so much more in life. Confront and acknowledge the things that you feel are holding you back. Whether it's overeating, overspending, over analyzing yourself and others, over thinking, or insecurities, release the anchor that is chaining you to one frame of mind. Ask yourself:

- What are these things feeding?
- What am I craving in my life?
- What emptiness am I using these things to fill?

Find out what it is and address it. We know the problems; we see the symptoms. Let's find the source and repair the damages.

Replace whatever was stolen. Fix whatever was broken. Learn whatever was missed and change whatever proved to be false.

WHAT YOU HAVE IS UNIQUE

It's a mental thing. Relationships with other women don't have to be difficult. Society has convinced us that we are a problem for ourselves and each other, that we are born jealous, selfish, attention seeking, emotional drama queens. The relationships that you see in those movies where women are so supportive of each other are happening. These relationships are occurring and being experienced in real life, in real time. It's just not happening in your life yet. Stop making excuses.

"Well, she said this about me last year."

"She's too this, or she's too that."

"I don't talk to her because my friend doesn't talk to her."

"I don't like her because she got the promotion that I should have gotten."

Let go of the grudges. Put down your grievances, forgive it, and release it. When you figure out who you are and what's meant for you, you find that there is no need to compete with any other woman. Her mission and yours are not the same. Even if you're both going after the same promotion at work or interested in the same guy, what she brings to that role will not be identical to what you can bring to it. So what if she got that promotion or that guy you like? It doesn't mean that you weren't good enough; it means that something else is out there for you, and that was for her.

Don't block your blessings by cursing someone else's. Don't sabotage the things that are on their way to you by pissing on the things that you already have. Change your mind about yourself in order to change your mind about other women. Your contribution may not be the same as anyone else's, but that doesn't diminish its value or the need for what you bring to the table. Sometimes it takes a few completely different moving parts to make something work, yet each individual part is of great importance.

Take a car, for example. For all the mechanics and intricate details and parts that go into building a car, without electricity or gas, it won't run. You may not be the steering wheel or the engine, but you may be that final missing piece that pulls it all together and makes it work. Sometimes your only role might be to see the potential in a woman and help her harness her greatness. Motivate her to go for it and help her succeed. Like a water faucet, it's full of potential. So much goes into getting that water from its primary source and out of that faucet, but until you turn that faucet on, it's only an object with potential. Stop underestimating your contribution. Don't disqualify yourself or another woman because you don't think that the hat you wear is big enough. Never trivialize what you can offer to the point it becomes insignificant. You are capable. Once you recognize your own greatness and you're able to tap into your strengths, you will flourish and want to see other women do the same.

We're usually at our best when we're most confident. It's that unexplainable quality that all women have, and it is the heart of where our sexiness lies. Can you believe that? Sexiness is actually on an equal playing field. It's not something that only some women have or can pull off, it's something inside of us all. It's not about the clothes you wear, the way you style your hair, or the amount of money you may have. Shake off all the negative crap they ever said about you. Let your voice be the one that matters most to you. Quiet that negative voice in your head with affirmations of love and appreciation. Record yourself saying wonderful things about who you are, who you want to be, and the amazing relationships you see yourself having. Start telling yourself a different story about you. Only you know all these incredible things about yourself. Think of one person you have helped in your life and one person who is grateful that you are a part of their life. Look at yourself in the mirror and know that no one can be you better than you can. Say it a thousand times as loud as you can. "I AM WORTH IT. I AM NOT PERFECT, BUT I AM ENOUGH AND I LOVE ME."

ADOPT A FEEL GOOD ATTITUDE

No one else can fill the purpose created for you. Start celebrating yourself, your life, your health, your family. Wear your clothes when you buy them. Rock that dress you love while watching tv on a Friday night. Put those heels on while you sit at your computer checking emails. Comb your hair and put on some makeup if that's what you like, even if you have no place to go. Don't wait for a special occasion. What's more special than the occasion of celebrating you?

Once in a while, treat yourself to some self-care and don't apologize for it. Have a party in the bathroom, "me, myself, and I." Put on your favorite song. Flirt with the mirror and enjoy yourself because you are gorgeous. Embrace all your flaws, whether you are big or small, no matter what color you are or where you come from. No matter what you've been through and who said what about you, embrace every story of your journey that you have lived to tell.

You are a survivor. Let everyone in your life know that you are working on you, so that you can be at your best for yourself and for them. You deserve to be celebrated, loved, and appreciated. Don't waste another second comparing yourself to another woman. Share your joy with her and help her find hers. Uplift and encourage one another. Never presume that another woman doesn't need to hear anything good from you. Don't assume she gets hundreds of compliments a day. It's not about quantity, it's about quality. A genuine compliment from one woman to another can smash one hundred shallow ones from a bunch of guys.

Once you love and accept yourself, you can focus on being the best version of you, not someone else. When you love yourself, it becomes much easier to love others. Don't shy away and feel shame over your imperfections. When you learn to embrace them, it allows you to be more accepting and compassionate toward others. When you stop pressuring yourself to be perfect, you pressure those around you less to live up to unrealistic expectations. The wonderful thing about it is that we all want to feel good. We want to be surrounded by people who also feel good about themselves and about us.

NOT SO DIFFERENT

Greatness takes on many forms. I look at my friend Shara for example, and I am so proud of her. My successful, intelligent, gorgeous, charismatic sister who only knows how to keep it 100 percent real all the time and she does it with class. She doesn't pretend to be anything she isn't. She uses all the greatness that makes her who she is to continue making the women in her life feel special.

There are so many women and girls who feel like they are invisible, that no one hears their voices or understands their pain. Right now, there is a woman being put down by a man. She's abused physically, psychologically, and emotionally. There is a woman being told that she's loved by her husband while he goes out and cheats on her. A young girl being told that being pretty makes her special, that her looks are all she has going for her. There is another being told that she is dumb and doesn't even have her looks to fall back on because she's ugly. There is a mother, a daughter, a sister, or a friend who feels like giving up because she has no help. She has no support, and she trusts no one to turn to. Meanwhile, there is another woman so in need of companionship that she trusts blindly. She suffers because of the hurt she's experienced far too many times.

There is a little girl questioning whether she should still be alive. She feels like an outcast and doesn't fit in. She hates herself because she doesn't look like the women on social media or on tv. On the other side, there is a young girl who's hated for being pretty even though she didn't create herself. There is a woman hearing that her body is not beautiful, and that she needs bigger breasts, hips, and thighs. Another hears that she needs to lose weight because her size makes her disgusting and unattractive. There is a girl who shows up at school every day with no food in her stomach. She's afraid to tell her classmates because they will tease her before they feed her. There is a woman walking miles for fresh water every day while another drives miles every day for chemotherapy. One is crying herself to sleep because she can't have children while another cries herself to sleep because she thinks she's failing as a mother.

There is a woman who is still in a toxic and dangerous relationship because she feels like that man is all she has. There is a girl who is keeping a secret of sexual abuse from surrounding women because she fears they will call her a whore, a slut, promiscuous, or easy. They will stone her with cruel words and judge the clothes she wears or how she lives her life instead of the person who took something from her. There is a woman who appears to have everything money can buy, but she is fading into the darkness of depression. She has no real friends in her life. Another woman is fighting a fatal illness while people snicker and pass judgment about her appearance or loss of her hair. There are women being sold, kidnapped, and kicked out into the streets. Women are held down in their careers, told that they cannot and should not dream any bigger. There are women punished for being women. They are not your competition; they are not your punching bags, your spectacles of mockery. They are your sisters in this life.

THERE IS RESPECT IN YOUR STRUGGLE

Stop beating yourself up over where you are in your life. Be grateful. We are blessed to have life. You're never too late for your purpose. Don't look at how far in front or behind someone else is. Focus on your pace. It's not always having more that makes others envy you; sometimes it's the light you bring to the world - the way you are, your core essence, how you treat others, and how others respond to you. Often, you're not being ridiculed, bullied, or looked down on because of what you don't have. It may be because of what you actually possess — those things that can't be bought, can't be touched, and cannot be destroyed or taken from you. No one can duplicate your virtues, characteristics, attitude, and energy. It's your vibe. Don't wait for others to believe in you. Believe in yourself. Do your best and be happy with your efforts, no matter who it does or doesn't impress. Practice getting excited about other people's wins. Let them know you recognize their positive attitudes and noble character - not only the women you know, but also the ones you don't.

If we removed the blinders from our eyes and really started looking at each other, we would realize that there is more that connects us than what separates us. There is an entire world out there hell bent on shoving us into categories — enjoying the amusement of the contest, convinced that we'd rather struggle to move a single tree on our own than put our differences aside and work together. They bask in the glory of our presumed defeat. They convince women that successful and peaceful collaborations are beyond our abilities, as if we're beautifully groomed dolls who lack intellect. They count on the fact that even though we know we're strongest when we stand together, we won't do what's necessary to achieve that togetherness. They cash in on the deeply rooted insecurities it creates in women only to serve their greed and deviant amusements. Women don't have to be pawns in this game any longer.

Speak up for the one who can't speak for herself. Act on behalf of the one who is still afraid. Love the one who hasn't figured out that she is worth loving yet. Respect the one who struggles to find self-respect. We are no better than those trying to degrade us and hold us back if we engage in the demise of one another. A simple circumstance shift based on a single life choice or chance moment can have you trading places with her in a matter of seconds. We don't have to be afraid of ourselves or each other. Put yourself out there. Let them see you; have no fear about who you are and whether they will like you. Make your contribution so impeccable that it is undeniable.

ADMIRATION, NOT COMPETITION

When your personal transformation makes those around you more inclined to do their best, that's not competition; that's inspiration. Own who you are and what your purpose is in your life and in the world. Own it every single day. When you see yourself and you realize and accept that you and she and I are different, that's the first step to overcoming the desire to compare and judge yourself and other women. The alternative is debilitating.

You are beautiful, amazing, and smart. If they don't like you, be brave enough to move through that negativity. You don't have to drink from the same poisonous glass. They haven't begun the work on themselves that you've started. Protect your heart, protect your mind, but be open. There are too few women being heard because they are shouting all by themselves. Together, women won't need to shout at all. We can shake the ground and create a thunderous echo of change that would be heard everywhere.

Now that I know I'm not the only woman who feels the pain I have suffered at different stages in my life, I can admit that I don't know if I could have handled the things that some other women have been through. My respect goes out to every woman for surviving her individual storm. No matter what you have, where you come from, or what your life looks like on the outside, I believe with certainty that you have survived something. You are a force of nature, even though different methods of nurture have manipulated, tricked, and shaped you. You are unique soldiers in the same army. Hold yourself and each other to higher standards. Stop preaching and start teaching. None of us are perfect and no one said change was going to be easy. Override that visceral fear. Take accountability for your actions and hold other women accountable as well. Be kind but firm in letting your sister know you see her, that you believe in her, you love her, and you only want the best for her. You shouldn't be so judgmental and critical of yourself. For the love of God, quit calling each other bitches, whores, and sluts. Quit vying for these crowns to sit as queen on thrones of female degradation. Don't miss out on the opportunity to learn, to be mentored, to grow with the help of another woman. Don't get clouded by the constant comparisons of where she is in her life as opposed to where you are.

Has anyone told you lately how gifted, wonderful, and beautiful you are? Well, you are. Believe it. Share it.

TEN
ENLIGHTENMENT

HAVE YOU EVER AWOKEN WITH AN IMMENSE FEELING OF GRATITUDE and excitement, thinking that today is the day when you start changing your life for the better? That's when you declare things like, "I will not get angry today. I'm going to be more patient, kinder, and more tolerant. I'm going to be a better person." Then by noon you're telling someone to go to hell.

Congratulations, you're human! It took more than a day for you to develop the habits you have now. Don't expect that you're going to wake up tomorrow and no other woman will ever get on your nerves again. Don't think that you're never going to criticize another woman again or tell her exactly what you think of her. No matter how much we change, it doesn't always mean that others will welcome the new you with a positive attitude. Don't expect everyone else to give you an easy time during your process. Don't even expect to be acknowledged for your strides in the right direction. It would be naïve of me to suggest that we try walking through life as saints, unprotected and completely oblivious to the monsters around us. Avoid the things and people that drain your soul. Surround yourself with those who fill you with love and support. Surround yourself with the women who are not threatened by you, but who respect and value you, the ones who want to see you do well and succeed.

WANT FOR YOUR SISTERS WHAT YOU WANT FOR YOURSELF

I must confess that even as I continue on my journey to becoming the best version of myself, it never eludes me that the intent is not perfection, but improvement. I fell prey to the idea that I needed to be Miss Perfect, Miss Congeniality, Miss Say-Yes-to-Everybody, and I couldn't risk anyone not liking me. After all, I had put so much work into being a better version of myself. Well, I could not keep that up, because people were taking advantage. People would do stupid or disrespectful things. People are going to test you.

Then they have the audacity to say, "Remember you're working on yourself."

"Uh, yes, I'm working on not losing my mind trying to keep my composure."

There were moments where I wanted to chime in on the daily gossip, situations where people would antagonize and push me to my limits just so they could see me break. I saw how amusing that was to some people - to see how much they could test my patience, only to give them the satisfaction of saying, "You haven't changed, you're just as bad as the women who bash other women."

I kept asking myself a simple question: "How does this course of action make me or her any better?"

When I think of my sisters, I think they are sometimes annoying, sometimes they get on my last nerve, sometimes they piss me all the way off. But guess what? I love them with all my heart. I would want nothing bad to befall them, even if we had a fight. If someone else tried to pick a fight with one of them, we'd put our differences aside. At that moment we are on the same team, ready to go to war together and for each other. Being able to look at other women in this same light and appreciate what they offer helped me navigate through those moments of impatience and anger. Jealousy and the desire to crush another woman's spirit, defame her character, or put her business in the streets added no value to my life. More than that, it would not make me feel good about myself.

The stories we fabricate and the rumors we spread can have lasting and damaging effects — not only to a woman's reputation, but also to her physical and emotional health. They could even affect her livelihood and her family. Hasten to believe the best in others and be apprehensive in believing the worst. A person sometimes only needs one person to believe in them.

The tongue can be an extremely poisonous instrument of hurt and pain. Words can inflict wounds so deep that even after they heal, the scars remain burnt into your psyche. However, the tongue can also be a source of healing, comfort, and restoration. You get to choose how you use it. Why is it we wait until someone is dying to care about their life as if being on death's doorstep provided us with that undeniable proof that they, too, were human all along? They feel, they hurt, they bleed, they cry, they struggle, and they suffer like we do. It shouldn't take life threatening or near-death experiences for us to reflect, to change, and step into who we actually are. If we can only achieve a speedy way to kindness by knowing that someone is dying, we should all wear labels on our foreheads that say that we are, in fact, each day growing closer to that inevitable truth. "We are all dying." Such dramatics aren't necessary, though.

What we love, we cherish. What we cherish, we respect and protect. It's not an impossible concept to turn to another woman, see some of yourself in her, and see her as a sister. If we only open our hearts, our minds, and our ears to one another, then all that distraction wouldn't deceive our eyes. Imagine this: I place a veil in front of you and ask every woman you've ever crossed paths with in your life to share her fears — her struggles, her pain, her hopes, and her dreams. You cannot see them, but you can hear them. You can hear their stories, their sorrows, joys, hurts, redemption, and happiness. The veil is lowered and you realize that all the women are wearing the same attire, so there is no distinction between the poor and wealthy. You're asked to match each story to the woman you think it belongs to. How well do you think you would do? It may surprise you to see who claims which of those stories and how many women claim the same stories. We all want the same things when it comes down to it: for ourselves and our families to be happy and healthy, for our children to be good, well-rounded, happy individuals, for our relationships to thrive. Everyone wants to be accepted and appreciated for who we are, to achieve our goals and live the life we have always wanted in happiness. We all want to be loved.

What I now want for myself is what I want for my sister. Being kind to other women doesn't make you weak. Trusting other women doesn't make you gullible. Believing that you can depend on other women doesn't make you delusional. Compassion and love don't mean you have to fix another woman's problems. Being present and supportive, creating a safe space of trust and not ridicule, is invaluable. All we need from each other is that thing called love.

THE PROCESS IS AN ONGOING ONE

You don't have to get this perfect, you only have to get started. Start with your friends, the ones you've harbored jealousies toward; your neighbor who you backbite because she's a homemaker and doesn't have a nine-to-five job; your co-worker who comes in daily and works her butt off without making friends because she hasn't had an easy go at any stage of her life, yet you try to turn others in the office against her; the girl who prepares your coffee at the coffee shop you frequent each day while you look down on her with insults if she makes a mistake; the lady at the register who you've never thought to ask how her day was going, even though she showed up to work with a sick child at home and a broken heart to be there to serve you; the school teacher you've envied because your child adores her for the attention she gives; the woman you talk about because she has an illness or contracted an STD; girls you belittle because they wear the same outfits over and over. Let your love pour. Let it flow from your veins one day at a time, one person at a time. To all the sideline spectators sitting back waiting for the next cat fight, name calling rant, the next backstabbing drama to occur within your collaborating team of women, well, they can kiss your collective backsides. You value each other's contributions. You respect and appreciate each other's differences. When a conflict occurs, you address it with your sister in a calm and mature manner. You handle it like the true intellects that you are.

I don't question for a second that it's in you. I don't doubt for a minute that you may have taken copious mental notes challenging my outlook on this. But this is my story. These are my feelings and I'm glad that I own them. I'm happy to claim them. When I bump into you, a stranger, you will receive the same love and sincerity that I would give to my sister. In my eyes, you are my sister. I don't care what you did yesterday, who you are, what you own, what you look like, what you believe, or where you come from. You deserve this love thing in all its capacity. Yes, you deserve to be heard and to be forgiven. You deserve to be treated with decency and respect - to be believed in and allowed the right to follow your dreams knowing that we, your sisters, are all rooting for you. You deserve to be happy. You may call me a hopeless dreamer and think that women will never stop the cat fighting, name calling, and competing for fame, power, and the attention and affection of men. I say you're wrong, and at the very least, let me dream.

We are soft, yet malleable. No one can make you strong; you do that. Strengthen your mind by first familiarizing yourself with it. Don't be a stranger to yourself. Take the time needed to work on you. Women are so much stronger than others perceive us to be. Contrary to popular belief, there are women all across the globe given due credit for fighting the good fight for their sisters — not to make a political statement or to gain fame. They are pushing forward to create a sisterhood using strength, acceptance, compassion, and understanding as their tools. Some are game changing, some life changing. They want for their sisters what they want for themselves and they are relentless in their fight. There are women out there teaching their sisters and helping them to achieve their goals. The notion that it's just who we are to feel jealousy, hatred, and resentment for each other is absolute horse crap. There is something incredible that happens when women create bonds with each other. The sisterhood of genuine friendship can be so powerful and meaningful that it ignites the light inside of you that you never even knew was there. That desire to love and to feel loved, that feeling that someone truly gets you - that's what it's about.

I spent so much of my life seeing far too many of these rivalries unfold. I've also seen orphaned little girls embracing each other, seeking solace and protection in the loving arms and companionship of each other. You are my sister, not my competition. I don't want your role in life. Your purpose is beyond me, as mine is beyond you. Like a cascade of dancing stars lighting up the night sky, so do all women shine beautifully together. Yet we still all have our moments in life where we shine brightest among the stars. When you step into your unique power and purpose, you radiate in a way unlike any other. Claim it, and when it's her turn, be happy, be gracious, an be kind. Allow each other to shine. Another woman's brightness doesn't diminish your light, it only adds more light to the darkness - the darkness of all the pain, suffering, and division in this world that breeds war and hate. You, woman! Yes, you. I'm talking to you! Your light is exactly what the world needs to pierce through it all, like a valiant bolt of lightning.

LOOK INSIDE

Although she's been with me my entire life, she got lost somewhere under all the pain and rubble. She is me and I needed to find myself. I needed to learn to love myself and allow myself to be loved the right way. When you've looked everywhere else for answers, prayed to God to help you find a way out, but you keep looking around and you can't seem to find the answer, when you feel you just don't know what else it's going to take, look to the place where you have not yet searched — yourself. The answer is within you. It was within me all along. The moment I began looking inward, the external factors were just a bunch of noisy distractions — a way to keep me from myself, to keep me from who I am and who I have the potential to become. I was blind to my power, to my value. I focused on the relationships that hurt me. I overlooked the ones where I was loved - and I am in fact loved, but not by the hundreds or the thousands that I thought were necessary to prove that I am special or worthy. I'm loved by a few who love me immensely, but not because I have done anything extraordinary. In their eyes, I am that extraordinary thing already.

A few months ago, my friend Mae and I had a misunderstanding. It had the potential to create a major conflict between us. I had hurt her feelings by expressing my dissatisfaction over something she had done for me. Mae responded in anger. I did not intend to offend her, even though she said my words were offensive. I initially rejected that conclusion. The more I tried to justify what I said and clarify my intent, the more upset and feistier she became. I didn't understand why she wouldn't just accept my clarification and apology and let it go.

What didn't occur to me at the moment was that my dismissal of her feelings really bothered her. I didn't acknowledge how she said I made her feel, since it was not my intention to hurt her feelings. Mae began firing back and pretty soon, it hurt my feelings as words were being exchanged. Then the insults just kept coming even after I backed off. At one point, I took a step back and reflected on the last insult she threw at me. I couldn't understand how something easily resolved became so personal and destructive. I had a choice to make — a choice that was much bigger than the moment or the issue that started it. The next words I used could either fracture the friendship or strengthen it. I said nothing for a while. Then I apologized to her for not hearing her out and for addressing my displeasure on such harsh terms.

Sure, I thought of an even more insulting comeback to her insult. I was angry. A part of me wanted to make her feel worse than I did -

but at what cost? I thought not only of who I am but also of who I know my friend to be. Despite what she was saying, I love her and I know she loves me. Even though I would prefer neither of us to have to live with the regret of saying something we didn't mean, there was only one thing I could control in that situation: myself. Making a conscious decision to exhaust every option in my head, I gave her every benefit of the doubt as to why she took it there. I reminded myself that my friend had a lot going on. She was struggling with depression and anxiety, and was in the middle of a huge and scary transition in her life. I used every excuse on her behalf. I told myself that there had to be a reason she was lashing out at me.

A few days later, Mae and I were discussing a cause dear to us. During that, she revealed she was struggling with guilt and hopelessness. She felt like she wasn't doing enough and she couldn't fix the greater social problem. She broke down in tears and told me she was sorry for lashing out at me and making me her punching bag that day. We told each other how much we value and love each other.

She said, "I should have known. We are always so connected even if we don't speak for days or weeks."

This is my friend, my sister. I know the goodness, the generosity, and the thoughtfulness of her. A moment of human emotion would not be enough to make me see her any other way. If I had opted to play tit for tat with insults, we would both be the losers. Always try to remember the best in others, exhaust every benefit of the doubt before concluding the worst. Remember that not everyone handles things the same way. Take a step back and ask yourself, "Do I want this relationship to survive this situation?" Being a bigger person doesn't make you weak. Lend your understanding and compassion to someone who may not be as strong as you are. I forgave my friend before she even apologized. In my mind, there had to be a why. Many times, it has nothing to do with you. No one wants to be on the receiving end of anyone's frustration-driven lapse in judgment. I'm not saying anyone should accept being a punching bag. Choose your battles. Be kind with your words. Take that step back. Have that moment and breathe. Know the power of your words. Understand that what motivates another person to use their words against you doesn't have to motivate you to do the same. Walking away from conflict when you know you have an arsenal that can inflict as much pain on the other person is not a straightforward thing to do. It will require all of your willpower.

TO HEAL, WE MUST FORGIVE

I could sit here all day and talk about how much the dynamic among women needs to change for the better. The actual change is within ourselves. That's really the only way to combat this. I needed to pause. I became good at making others feel good about themselves while I was falling apart. That led to a lot of deflecting, passing my insecurities off onto others to lessen the pain. I hadn't reflected and gotten to the source, the root of the problem. Then one day an overwhelming wave of emotions devoured all my senses.

My friend Javi said to me during one of our more intense conversations, "JJ, forgive in order to let it go."

Forgiveness? I used to think that forgiveness had to be earned. I was wrong. People work to earn things for themselves, things that benefit them. I am still baffled by what overcame me, but it registered in not only my mind, but also in my heart. Now, I was finally ready and willing to follow through. In that moment, I realized all the previous years of working on myself had led up to that epiphanic moment. I needed to forgive them for myself. I needed to free myself. The damage was done, but I was still standing and stronger than ever.

I first had to heal and forgive myself for the grudges I once carried, for the resentments that spawned insecurities and for the self-doubt I dragged with me for so long. Then I needed to forgive them all: everyone and anyone who has ever said or done anything to hurt me, to break me, belittle me, bully me, or criticize me. I released them from the blame and responsibility. None of us are perfect and it's this common fact that should make us more understanding of each other.

Every day requires you to work on yourself. Mind your own business and not spread salacious, slanderous, damaging rumors about others. Help another person when you see her in need. Lift your friends. Encourage and cheer on your co-workers to do their best. Motivate and inspire the women around you and be gracious and kind toward strangers. Take responsibility and be mindful of the examples being set for the children. Every day requires work. If I do it, you do it, she does it, and we all do it, we can establish a universal sisterhood where women feel less judged and misunderstood by one another. We can't allow the way we look, where we come from, what we believe in, or what we have accumulated in wealth, status, or fame to define or divide us — love and our desire for happiness, health, and success are all things that should unite us.

LET'S HAVE EACH OTHER

Go shake off those labels and preconceived ideas about who you are and who we all are as women. Let's change the narrative and rewrite the story. Give young girls more women to look up to, more mentors they can trust. Let's teach them they can compete in education and sports. They can go for that position in the school play or at their job — even for the presidency of a country. They can rise and change the world and do it all while still respecting, admiring, and supporting the women going after these same dreams. Let's teach them that healthy competition is alright without producing hateful rivalry. It's not, "may the best woman win." It's, "may the woman whose time is now capture her blessing."

Each of our times will come. If another woman gets there before you do, she can help you get there even faster. She can teach you, guide you, and support you along your journey. Let's teach these young women that they do not have to compete for the attention of men. The men aren't going anywhere. The one that's meant for you will find you. He might miss you if the real you is hidden behind your attempts to be more like someone else. Let's create a society where, when they write about women collaborating with each other or women in the workplace, they have to come up with a new set of adjectives to describe the phenomenon — sisters, no longer rivals. You are my sister; she is your sister. We are all sisters, not each other's competition.

There are so many beautiful parts to you, to us all. Practice makes improvements, not perfection. There will always be room to grow. We can't ever stop listening to each other, learning from each other, and trying to be better human beings. We may never get this all the way right, but we must keep trying every day to treat each other in the right way - in a loving, sisterly way. Who knows how long we have left to stay? We can and need to do this and we need to do it now. How do you wish to change the world? Let's change it today, one woman at a time. Let's grab our brushes, use our favorite color and unique flair, and let's paint the world the most unbelievable shade of love that it's ever seen.

ELEVEN
IT'S JUST A LOVE THING

FOR THIS TO WORK, ALL WE HAVE TO DO IS TRY. WE HAVE TO SEE who we become when we live by a common code — love. It's not an optional factor in this. It is the answer. Hate is often the hardest habit to break, but love is the hardest thing to do.

Our success in this requires a few steps:

RELATE

We're too disconnected and out of touch with the basic nature of who we all are as human beings. Look at another person and realize that they are no different from you; they too have value, people they care about and who care about them. They have goals and desires. They want to feel safe and loved too. The moment we start looking at people as humans instead of 'other' or 'less than,' we begin to see the common threads that connect us. It allows us to see not only the other person, but ourselves. Realize that through our experiences with others and how much we have in common, we inevitably learn about ourselves. This brings us to the second point.

REFLECT

Looking inward can be terrifying. It can be a confrontation unlike any other. Accept that this is a necessary step and commit to being completely honest with yourself. Who we are will always catch up with us, no matter how far or how fast we try to run from ourselves. Before you can face the sources of your resentments, jealousies, and hatred, you must first be aware that there is a problem. Examine your own attitudes and insecurities. Write them down if you need to. Now, this doesn't mean that your attention should be focused only on the negative things that need to be worked on. Spend time diving into the best parts of yourself as well and continue sharpening those areas, because the negative things said and done to us can often occupy space in our thoughts longer than they should. This is an ongoing process and it will require awareness, focus, patience, consistency, and, most of all, honesty. This is pivotal to the next step.

RESET

Don't live in the past; put it behind you and commit to your self-growth now.

Take responsibility and be prepared to hold yourself accountable moving forward. Acknowledge that although you may be a victim, you may also be a perpetrator of these behaviors. Apologize. Make amends with those you have hurt and request forgiveness without expectations. It's also necessary to create a plan for change. How are you going to repair things? Write it down. This plan must not only include how you will repair the damage you've caused others, but also how to heal the damage caused to you. Once you've done that, all that's left is to follow through. Remember that whatever you uncover about yourself, it does not have to be your permanent state. By resetting, you allow yourself to change, improve, and grow. The journey to your best self is infinite. Loving yourself no matter where you are in this process is key.

Love strips us down, opens us up, and leaves us vulnerable. It can be painful and we want to be exempt from that pain and suffering, but love also heals those wounds. Love creates bridges, not barriers. It allows us to do the impossible and connects us all on the most human and spiritual levels.

It's unacceptable, the world which we have designed and are leaving for young people. They are ill-equipped to clean up the messes we have made and take on figuring this shit out. Many young people are choosing to live inside their own heads, shutting everyone out. They are afraid and feel alone. They keep secrets from those closest to them because they don't feel like they can trust us. We have created a dynamic of distrust.

We must quit imposing standards and rules that we ourselves don't live up to or follow. We can't keep preaching to them not to question our authority, to do as we say and not as we do. The messages we're sending confuse them more than anything else. When faced with decisions that could have permanent consequences in their lives, they make them without us. We try to protect them from the monsters in life: the strangers, the bad boys, the dangerous men, the drugs and alcohol. What about us? Who will protect them from the harmful and misguided biases we carry? Who will protect them from the influences that dictate our lives and trickle into theirs? We can and we will. It's time we rectify the problem.

WE ARE OUR SISTERS' KEEPER

There are drills carried out in schools meant to prepare students for the worst-case scenario — if someone enters the school to threaten or take their lives. There are no drills to prepare them for when someone threatens or destroys their will to live. Too many women and girls are no longer with us. We don't want to hear about another young girl taking her own life because of bullying. We are our sisters' keepers. Don't ignore each other's cries anymore. Suffering in silence is killing our women. Anxiety and depression are real. No one wants to live in a state of feeling like they have no control over their emotions. I plead with you to show up when another woman feels like she is not worth loving. Show up for the woman who feels that she is not enough and is unworthy of being cared for. Show up for the woman who never allows herself to feel that pain by convincing herself that she shouldn't love and doesn't deserve love herself, because there is nothing lovable about her. We are our sisters' keepers.

Dash away the self-doubt and replace it with confidence. Don't forget those scars that also made you who you are. Accept the past, but don't allow it to control you and make you reactive to the feelings and opinions of others. We prejudge others and situations. We expect the worst outcome based on our preconceived notions and decide to give that person a chance or not, like them or not, and expect the worst from them or not. Think of a fan that you've just taken to the electrician because you say it doesn't work. What's the first thing the electrician does? He or she plugs it into an electrical source to confirm your claim. The fan works now and you realize that the reason it didn't before was because you didn't plug it in. Every time you're looking at a problem, think of the simplest solution first. Begin small and don't overthink things. Get to know an individual instead of categorizing based on stereotypes. Your experiences happened to you; they are what you overcame, not who you are.

Being sexy, looking expensive, seeking attention, and being boastful or bitchy is easy. Being ourselves is much more to lose. It's easy to let go of something that is fake. When it's you, the real you, it's much more difficult to change the fundamental core of who you are. After reflecting, we must reset. We are not perfect and we don't have to be perfect to steer someone else in a better direction.

We can't stop and we can't give up. We have to keep putting in the work every day and allow that love to drive us. Be honest with yourself and in identifying your own problems. Choose to forgive people even though they hurt you. Replace that resentment and hate with love. Let's host more gatherings in our communities where we can all meet and get to know one another. Let's ask those co-workers out to lunch and introduce ourselves. Let's mentor other women and be a positive example of a big sister to a young girl. I do not believe in role models. None of us are perfect, and it's better to encourage and inspire someone to be the best version of themselves rather than a version of anyone else. Let's do this! We can look for the good in each other and complement one another. We don't need to fish for compliments from men to confirm our worth. You are worth it! We all are! We are magnificent and we are enough.

SOME WOMEN ARE JEALOUS OF AND FRUSTRATED WITH OTHER women, but are mostly frustrated with themselves because that woman makes it look too easy and she's exhibiting standards you find impossible to achieve or maintain. Slow down and embrace the softer side of who you are, those qualities that make your radiance unique - your integrity, humility, intellect, charm, and charity. Take the time to admire the wonder of yourself. You give so much to the world, but you must also water your own seed for it to blossom. Self-love is also about taking the time to check in with yourself. Relax and reset your thoughts. Get your spiritual, physical, and mental health in check. Set some time aside to pamper and beautify yourself. You set your standards and at the risk of sounding like a broken record, your only competition is you.

There are girls being born every day, a few thousand as you read this sentence. There is no need to compare yourself with who's younger, prettier, or more successful. God has given you this incredible gift of life and you alone possess all the things that make you, you. No one can take that away from you. No other woman, no matter how young or old, rich or poor, can ever be you. Stop feeling sorry for yourself and angry at other women who have found peace. The only difference between them and you is that they are not looking at you. They are too busy enjoying who they are. Give each day your best. Don't overwork yourself into the ground. Don't lose your femininity by chasing after material things. There's nothing wrong with hard work and having goals. However, if you're working tirelessly just to have a more expensive pair of shoes, car, or purse to keep up with another woman, is the goal really worth it if you are miserable, exhausted, and hating yourself for not having the time or energy to do the things that really make you happy? By the time you've got these things, the woman you are competing with or the man you are competing over has moved on to something different , leaving you feeling defeated, hopeless, and depressed. Dash away the self-doubt and replace it with confidence.

You don't need anyone's permission to be happy. When you understand your intrinsic worth, it's easy to love yourself. When you love yourself, it's easy to love others.

If you are already there, then it's time to take another woman into your fold. Mentor a young girl. Seek ways and opportunities to work alongside other women. Share in each other's happiness and comfort each other through the struggles. Help other women to problem solve instead of criticizing them for not figuring it out yet. Celebrate their efforts and achievements and be an advocate and defender when it's most needed.

Love is the essential missing piece. I challenge you to love. Love yourself, love each other, love harder, love better, love more than you have ever loved before. This is a matter of saving lives - not just now or tomorrow, but every day.

We can no longer seek to shroud our insecurities with superficial distractions living in a society based on class, where merits are not based on what your mind offers, but what you look like, who you are, where you come from, and what you have. It's okay to feel lost. It's okay to feel scared, confused, defeated, and uncertain. The good news is that no group of people holds dominion over the peace inside of you. No one has a monopoly over talent, hard work, and determination. Keep doing your best and you will manifest what you think about most. Forget about all that didn't happen for you and focus on all that's about to happen for you.

We all have a role to play in this bigger picture called life. Sometimes it will be up to you to see that thing within another person that makes them great, even if they haven't seen it yet. We have to believe in the potential of each other to do good. All we have to do is try. Once we know who we are, it becomes easier to see who we might become. All we have to do is take that first step. Acknowledge the problem and confront the rightful source of the issues.

There are two hungers within each of us. Choose the one you wish to feed. Remember that love for yourself is the key to loving others - not arrogance, just genuine appreciation for who you are, your self-worth, recognition that you have a purpose, and acceptance that you are capable of just doing your personal best and being happy with it all. You are all that and much more. You are capable of giving and receiving love.

We cannot be okay encouraging class separation based on the color of people's skin, where they live, or how much money they have. None of this is alright. It is so much easier to be angry — to hate, resent, and hurt others. Love is much harder, because love leads to an inevitable pain in one form or another. We have to change the narrative, even if it may not be a universally acceptable one.

There will be times when we're going to make the process hellishly hard for each other. There will be times when we question ourselves and each other. We can give a million dollars to female charities. That still doesn't mean we'll never experience feelings of jealousy or resentment toward a woman. That doesn't make us horrible people, though. We have so much that binds us and, believe it or not, we're terribly unoriginal when it comes down to what we all truly want in this life: to live, to be free, safe, secure, healthy, and happy.

At the end of it all, it's those tough experiences which create those cool edges that add to our unique and impeccable strength. They help shape us and enrich our lives. Don't be so afraid to admire another woman that you allow your pride to muddy it with jealousy. We don't need to feel like we're simply surviving among each other. Let's change that and live, because the harsh yet simple reality is this: If we can't love, then we can't heal. If we can't heal, then we can't move forward. If we can't move forward, then we can't make things better, and if we can't make things better, then we're all fucked.

You are not just strangers or anonymous faces behind a screen. You are a woman, a girl, my spouse's ex-girlfriend, my classmate, my colleague, my teacher, my boss, or even a friend. You are phenomenal, worthy, enough, and irreplaceable. You are my sister and we need you. I love you. Now love yourself and show the world who you are by ending the cycle of female rivalry and replacing it with love and appreciation for one another. Straighten your crowns, put on your heels, lace up your sneakers or boots, or put on your flip-flops and let's do this.

ACKNOWLEDGMENTS

There comes a point in every woman's life when she must reflect on those who have paved the way for her. She must give recognition to the ones who helped mold the beautiful mind she now shares. This is that point for me .

I thank God for my mother, who has always been such a warrior. There is much that can and should be said about you, mother, but that would need its own separate book. You are exceptional at being my mother. Your love is unparalleled and you remain my greatest inspiration. To complete this book in your lifetime and in your honor has been an absolute privilege. I only hope that you are as proud of me as I am of you. There is no number of heavy-handed words or phrases that could ever sum up the magnitude of my love, respect, admiration, and appreciation for you. You taught me how to be humble, kind, compassionate, and generous. You showed me through example what hard work, self-respect, and integrity look like. I love vigorously and forgive without being asked because of you. You taught me the beauty and the blessing in being independent, while still needing and relying on those we love. You taught me to have manners and appreciate others because no one can do it alone. You gave me the best of you, and you are the best part of me. I love you immensely and infinitely mommy.

Auntie Noreen, you knew that you wanted to play a part in my life before I was even born. You were determined to protect and help care for me. I remember the first time I traveled with you at eight years old and couldn't wait to get back home to my mom. You spanked me for not eating my veggies, for crying and running away from getting my hair combed, and for not tidying up after myself. I thank you for that. Whenever someone tells me that I'm always in the kitchen, that I'm a clean freak, or that I eat like a rabbit and there's too much green food in my refrigerator, I always smile and think how proud you would be. I love you so very much. You've always been there with an unwavering love and an abundance of support. For that, I thank you.

Miss Sandra, or Mama Sandra, you held onto me from the very moment you first saw me as a child. I have always loved you for the love, generosity, and respect you showed to me and my mom. I remember spending weekends at your house, where you encouraged me to read. You were relentless in ensuring that I did my homework. You saw the light and talent in me, and never wanted that to be abused or exploited. You continue to be a rock of strength, wisdom, and encouragement whenever I need it. Your voice never leaves me: "Be yourself, be who you are, and love who you are. Don't let anyone else tell you who you are." For these words, your genuine love and support, and so much more, I love you.

I thank the women who encouraged and emboldened me to take this brave step forward, inspiring me from near and far. My amazing South African family, Andrea, Miss Yvonne, and Miss Delia: You three will never understand how much meeting you has changed my life. My teachers, Mrs. Samuel, Ms. Daniel, and Mrs. Anthony, all taught me at three very crucial stages in my life and education. You each instilled the discipline and encouragement I needed to thrive. You never gave up on me. Thank you for protecting me and nurturing my mind.

To my sisterhood of phenomenal women — Monique, Chantelle, Glennica, Denorda, Kenya, Shacka, Verslyn, and Bettyann - you are engraved on my heart, and no distance or time has managed to sweep you away. You have been consistent and steadfast in your love and support. You are the rarest of gems; I love and thank you for choosing me as your friend, and for teaching me through your experiences. Thank you for always sharing your knowledge, laughs, and wisdom with me. Each of you has saved me in some way at some point . We can speak for minutes or for hours; so much time can pass between us and still it's as though we never lost a minute. Our experiences, joys, and pains are so parallel that it humbles me to know each of you, and to be understood and appreciated by you. You will forever have my love and gratitude. You are vital parts of the family I chose.

My cousins Alicia and Brontie have both been there through the most difficult times. Alicia, you are my vault. There is nothing I can't tell you. Thank you for your loyalty, trust, and wisdom. You are beautiful, patient, generous, and one of the funniest and kindest women I know. I am so blessed to have you in my corner. Brontie, you have always been an incredible voice of reason, compassion, and understanding. Thank you for always supporting me, encouraging me, and showing up for me. You both deserve the happiest of lives. I love you.

My friend and sister, Sarah. All I can say is that you are a light in the darkness. I thank God that you're here and I'm so blessed to be able to call you friend and sister. You are my sounding board and your input is always a much-needed treat. Girl, thank you for putting up with me and for being you. You remain one of my greatest assets.

Diana, you are a diva in the best way — crazy, fabulous, and fun. My bestie. Like a pearl, you present a tough exterior and though you are one of the strongest women I know, what lies beneath is a sensitive, loyal, kind, and generous woman. It brings me such pleasure to have been your friend and sister for over 20 years now. We are sisters by choice and by heart, and I love you for taking me as I am. Thank you for always having my back and for all your unwavering love, honesty, and support. You are an incredible source of laughter, strength, and love, and I look forward to sitting on that porch as old ladies laughing about the incredible journey we've been blessed to take together.

My youngest sister Bless - that's what we call you - you truly are a blessing. You're all grown up now, and I am so proud of you. I wrote this book hoping to offer you some guidance as you venture out on your own path to self-discovery. You will come to face your own hardships, but always treat others well. Remember where you came from and that your truest and purest form of beauty comes from inside you. I admire your confidence and self-assurance, and I hope you never lose that part of yourself. I love you sweetheart.

To Saskia and Arianna, sometimes it takes more than biology to make a family. Thank you for accepting me as your sister by heart. You have my gratitude for bringing your lights of energy, love, innocence, and beauty into my family's life. You motivate me to be a better woman and a better example. I love, respect, and appreciate you for the nonstop and incomparable work you do in raising my youngest nieces. Thank you for your love, support, and encouragement. May God's grace, wisdom, mercy, and guidance walk you further toward being the best women and mothers that you can be. You are loved, appreciated, and beautiful.

Hailee, my lioness sister-in-law, you have managed to make me love you in such a short time. Your laugh is infectious. I do believe that you are the only woman suited to handle my brother's ridiculousness and sense of humor . You add so much joy to this family. Your love and devotion have been incredible to witness. I know you don't think so, nor would you admit it, but you are the definition of a super mom. You are doing a fantastic job, sis, and it is more than enough for us. Thank you for your open heart, moral guidance, support, and love. I love and appreciate you and I'm honored to call you sister.

Although this book is about women, it would be remiss of me not to mention the men who have contributed in one way or another.

My cousin Kevin, you have been a friend, brother, father, and counselor wrapped in one. You have looked out for me ever since the day we met. My love for you is immeasurable. You have never disappointed me, even when you haven't agreed with me. Thank you for the countless hours of conversation, which often provided me with the best ideas. Thank you for always encouraging me to go for it and to see where all roads would lead. Thank you for seeing the greatness in me even when I didn't see it in myself. I am honored and humbled at the thought of having you always in my corner. You make me unafraid to try, unafraid to be myself, and unafraid to allow myself to just be happy. I love and appreciate you from my soul and I thank God for placing you in my life.

To my big brother Wayne: Never has a sister been so blessed to have a big brother care so much for her best interest. You gave me a deadline of one weekend during my procrastination phase to finish writing this book, refusing to let me continue writing in peace if I didn't meet that deadline — Ha! Thank you for allowing me the space and freedom to work. Writing can sometimes be an isolating process. Thank you for understanding when I only surfaced for food and water, and you didn't see me or hear a word from me all day. You have supported me throughout this process and encouraged me to keep going, to see this all the way through no matter the outcome. You will never know how truly appreciated you are. I love you immensely big bro.

My brothers Jason, Swanday, and Bernel (BJ), you are my soldiers and my motivation. I am so proud of each of you for charting your own path in life. My only hope is that you remain focused on your goals and be the best fathers and men that you can be. Thank you for always respecting me, loving me, and believing in me. I love and adore you dearly.

Heartfelt thanks and love to my nephews Dimitri, Trey, and Kayden who inspired me and kept me smiling throughout the process; to my writing coach Michelle and the staff at SPS for their time and excellent resources; to my amazing editor, formatter, and mentor Jaclyn, my cover designers, and my awesome launch team. Thank you all from the bottom of my heart. You truly helped me bring it all to life.

None of this would be possible without The Creator whose grace, mercy, and guidance helped me put pen to paper and bring dreams to reality. May the almighty God continue to bless me, and may he continue to bless you.

ABOUT THE AUTHOR

J. A. Huggins is a Caribbean born Aquarius and philanthropist who lives in Orlando, Florida. She is a health-conscious foodie who first developed a love for the arts and began writing poetry at age nine. After undergoing a heartbreaking surgery in 2016 and then traveling to South Africa three months later on a journey that would forever change her life, she has since been determined to challenge the divisive paradigm of female relationships within her own life and promote change in the lives of as many women as she can reach.

THANK YOU FOR READING MY BOOK

I really appreciate all of your feedback, and I love hearing what you have to say.

I need your input to make the next version of this book and my future books better.

Please leave me an honest review on Amazon letting me know what you thought of the book.

Thanks so much!

J. A. Huggins

www.ingramcontent.com/pod-product-compliance
Lightning Source LLC
Chambersburg PA
CBHW060456280326
41933CB00014B/2770